D0752427

Totally
Tyra:
An Unauthorized Biography

by Lila Chase

PRICE STERN SLOAN
Published by the Penguin Group
Penguin Group (USA) Inc., 375 Hudson Street,
New York, New York 10014, U.S.A.
Penguin Group (Canada), 90 Eglinton Avenue East, Suite
700, Toronto, Ontario, Canada M4P 2Y3
(a division of Pearson Penguin Canada Inc.)
Penguin Books Ltd, 80 Strand, London WC2R 0RL, England
Penguin Ireland, 25 St Stephen's Green, Dublin 2, Ireland
(a division of Penguin Books Ltd)
Penguin Group (Australia), 250 Camberwell Road,
Camberwell, Victoria 3124, Australia
(a division of Pearson Australia Group Pty Ltd)
Penguin Books India Pvt Ltd, 11 Community
Centre, Panchsheel Park, New Delhi - 110 017, India
Penguin Group (NZ), Cnr Airborne and Rosedale Roads,
Albany, Auckland 1310, New Zealand
(a division of Pearson New Zealand Ltd)
Penguin Books (South Africa) (Pty) Ltd, 24 Sturdee
Avenue, Rosebank, Johannesburg 2196, South Africa

Penguin Books Ltd, Registered Offices:
80 Strand, London WC2R 0RL, England

Photo credits: Cover: copyright CBS/Photofest. Insert: first page, courtesy of Photofest; second page, (top) copyright © Dominick Conde/Star File, (middle) copyright © Dominick Conde/Star File, (bottom) copyright CBS/Photofest; third page, (top) copyright CBS/Photofest, (bottom) copyright UPN/Photofest; fourth page, copyright © Dominick Conde/Star File.

Cover and interior design by Michelle Martinez Design, Inc.

Library of Congress Control Number: 2006007239

ISBN 0-8431-2121-1   10 9 8 7 6 5 4 3 2 1

Totally Tyra:

An Unauthorized Biography

by Lila Chase

PSS!
PRICE STERN SLOAN

Contents

Introduction

"Lightbulb head" and "Olive Oyl." It might be hard to believe, but these were the cruel nicknames that Tyra Banks often heard from classmates while growing up in Los Angeles, California. Of course, the stunning green-eyed goddess eventually showed the people who taunted her about her incredibly large forehead, Amazon-like height, and scrawny weight (five-foot nine and ninety-eight pounds at age eleven) by becoming one of the highest-paid supermodels in the 1990s and achieving several big firsts for an African American model in her career.

Tyra's extraordinary success in life stems from her natural grace and charisma, coupled with an incredible work ethic and willingness to prepare for everything. She even understands the importance of listening to her mother when she offers her wise advice. Tyra also knows how to be relentless when it comes to going after what you want. At first, she was rejected from six agencies because they didn't think she was photogenic enough to be a model. Tyra didn't give up, though, and after she got her big break, she dazzled the fashion world with her spunk and personality.

She was the first model ever to receive twenty-five invitations to walk the runway during her first attempt at the fall haute couture shows in Paris. (Models typically get three.) In 1996, she was the first female to appear on the cover of *GQ*, a popular men's magazine, and, a year later, the first African American to grace the cover of the legendary *Sports Illustrated* swimsuit issue. Enviable contracts with Cover Girl Cosmetics and Victoria's Secret lingerie made her a household name. She even won the Michael Award for Supermodel of the Year in 1997, the equivalent of winning the Oscar in her industry.

The sassy star wasn't content to stop there. First, she branched out into acting, sharing screen time and love scenes with Will Smith—the Fresh Prince himself—and *Felicity*'s Scott Foley on TV. She even starred with a little known redheaded actress named Lindsay Lohan in a made-for-TV movie. Tyra's film debut was in the acclaimed drama *Higher Learning*, directed by John Singleton, her boyfriend at the time. She has a lot more roles on her resume than the usual model-turned-actress, but Tyra's true strength lies in just being Tyra in front of the camera.

In 2003, Tyra took on reality TV, creating, producing, and starring in *America's Next Top Model*—an up-close and personal look at the super-competitive and glamorous world of modeling. It has become one of the most successful reality shows on TV today—in large part because of Tyra's heart and grit.

Now Tyra is practically the Oprah Winfrey of the next generation since launching her own talk show in the fall of 2005. She appears to be having a great time interviewing celebrities and real people, tackling serious issues like body image and bad breakups plus fun extras, like fashion for dogs.

Tyra considers her most important job as being a role model to young girls across the country. She's never forgotten her earlier years of insecurity and low self-esteem. She's made it her mission to use her celebrity platform to remind girls that their beauty on the inside matters as much as their beauty on the outside. And what really makes a girl shine is personality, perseverance, and the ability to be comfortable in her skin.

Sure, Tyra is absolutely, utterly, drop-dead gorgeous. But Tyra's best asset is being her goofy, candid self. Though Tyra is undeniably beautiful and, in her own words, "fierce," it's clear that she is *much* more than just a pretty face!

Chapter 1
Growing Up Insecure

*T*yra Lynne Banks was born on December 4, 1973. Her parents, Donald, a computer consultant, and Carolyn, a medical photographer at NASA, raised her and her older brother, Devin, in LA's Inglewood section, a close-knit, middle-class, predominantly black community. Although Donald and Carolyn divorced when Tyra was six years old, Donald has always remained close to the entire family.

Fortunately, the divorce didn't make things difficult for Tyra. To this day, she approaches the issue with her typical glass-half-full philosophy. "To be quite honest, I was too young to be hurt, scared, or upset in any way. As far as I could see, I had it made. I had two birthday parties, two Christmases. Double the presents, double the love," Tyra said.

Even though she always had her parents' support, Tyra swears she didn't hear that she was pretty for most of her youth. When she was about nine, she suffered from various skin ailments, including a horrible chronic case of warts. She would constantly hide her hands in her pockets and go as far as wearing gloves in the middle of summer. It made her feel very self-conscious.

It was impossible to hide her height, which made her stand out in a way she didn't want to at all. Her gawky look prevented people—including herself—from seeing her prettiness potential.

Tyra remembers puberty as particularly painful. "I had no self-esteem." She told *Shape* magazine that she was a "geeky adolescent . . . braces, tall. Kids would tease me. I would go home crying all the time."

Things only got worse for Tyra at first. She told *GQ* magazine that unlike most models, who exaggerate and say they weren't attractive when they were kids, she truly was the ugly duckling in the beginning of junior high school. "Big eyes, big braces, and I always had food stuck in them. And I was chubby."

That is, until she lost nearly 20 pounds over one summer. Then she says, "I was ninety-two pounds and five-foot nine in eighth grade. People called me Olive Oyl, Lightbulb Head, and Fivehead, because my forehead was so big." Tyra was horrified to realize she was even taller than her teacher. "I was thin as a rail and miserable."

At eleven, she weighed only ninety-eight pounds, and some people even worried about her health. Tyra told a Florida paper that her height "was a growth spurt, not a disease, but they stuck me with needles for a year to see if I was sick."

Tyra felt so self-conscious about her body that she mostly kept to herself and didn't try to make friends. "Before all these bizarre physical changes, I was extroverted, had a lot of friends, and was always in trouble for trying to show off and be the class clown. When I lost the weight and grew so tall, I became self-conscious and introverted. I'd do anything to avoid the rude stares of people. I rarely showed my face in public, and when I did, it was buried in a book."

All that reading and studying paid off when Tyra was accepted to Immaculate High School, a prestigious Catholic girls' school in the Los Feliz section of Los Angeles. The teasing didn't go away at the school—"All the girls would laugh at me when I walked by. I wasn't just skinny and tall; I was sick looking. If anybody called me skinny, I would just smile, then run into my room and cry." But Tyra received a great education, for which she will always be grateful.

Immaculate High School is also where Tyra first heard about modeling. Kehfri, a fellow student, walked up to Tyra and told her she looked like a model. "I was surprised because she was a really attractive girl who became a local model—the first person to tell me that." Still, Tyra, went home, took a long look in the mirror, and decided she "was still awkward, with the thin, long-legged body of a ballerina, track runner, or basketball player."

Tyra's family also realized that she was actually turning into quite a beauty, so her mom convinced her to give modeling a try when she was in twelfth grade because it would allow her an opportunity to see the world.

Believe it or not, Tyra never dreamed of becoming a model. At one time, she wanted to be a veterinarian, but after seeing her first movie, she fell in love with the idea of becoming a filmmaker. "The first movie I ever saw was *The Wiz*, when I was five or six. I was so amazed. I wanted to make something like that." And Tyra always loved performing. One of her favorite pastimes while growing up was to buy makeup at Thrifty's, a local store, and vogueing with friends in her mom's high heels and long robes around her family's Inglewood duplex.

So Tyra put a portfolio of pictures together—with the help of her photographer mom—and hit the modeling agencies in LA. At first, Tyra met with nothing but rejection. "All the agencies said I wasn't photogenic. I had people tell me that I'm 'too black, not black enough, lips are too big, forehead too big,' just so many things."

In fact, at the time that Tyra was first breaking into the modeling world, there weren't that many African American models who worked steadily. Beverly Peele, Iman, and Naomi Campbell had all made it, but cosmetic companies were looking for more "all-American" faces to represent their campaigns. So Tyra was in for a challenging, uphill battle!

She did succeed in getting a little bit of work at local department stores like JC Penney's, but she didn't feel that she was getting any closer to her "big break." Eventually, Tyra dropped her runway plans for the time being and applied to colleges to study film. Five colleges accepted her, and Tyra chose to attend Loyola Marymount University, which was only 20 minutes from her hometown.

Tyra was disappointed that modeling didn't work out, but this shy, wholesome bookworm was eager to start school. Maybe she'd even play basketball—which had been a dream of hers since her father first introduced her to the sport as a child.

Donald Banks often took a young Tyra to watch the Lakers play at the Staples Center, and she became a huge fan. "My dad taught me to play when I was a kid because I was so tall for my age," Tyra told *InStyle* magazine.

Tyra's height didn't make athletic ability a forgone conclusion, however. By the time she was nine, she had sprouted to five-foot eight, making her a perfect candidate for the basketball team. Yes, Tyra always made the team. She just didn't get to play the game. "I was so clumsy and uncoordinated that I eventually became the official benchwarmer. I couldn't shoot to save my life. So unless we were way ahead or hopelessly behind, I didn't see much court time. I was a lost cause!"

(Despite that frustration, Tyra has never lost her affection for the game. Even after becoming a huge star in the modeling world, she jokes that she would give up modeling to be a basketball star. "It's nice to have people say, 'You're so pretty,' but I'd love to hear, 'Girl, that layup was fine.'")

Now that modeling was on hold, however, maybe she finally had a shot at scoring on the court!

Just two weeks before classes started, though, fate stepped in, and Tyra's life changed forever.

Chapter 2

Tyra Takes Paris!

*A*fter being rejected by four top modeling agencies, Tyra had struck pay dirt—the Elite modeling agency wanted to sign her! At the time, Tyra had no idea that this was to be the start of a record-breaking modeling career. "An agent saw pictures of me and said I was the only girl she wanted to take back to Paris," she said. "I didn't leave thinking I was going to be some big fashion model. I just wanted to make money for college."

The woman who had seen Tyra's picture through Elite was Veronique, a French talent scout for a company called City Models. Veronique recommended that Tyra postpone college and model for the couture fashion houses in Paris. Tyra was finally on her way!

Tyra's story shows that you can never give up on a dream. "There's a lot of people who will tell you no," Tyra once said to *Jet* magazine. "One agency said yes. All you need is for one person to say yes."

For Tyra, it was just the foot in the door that she needed.

The opportunity to work the runway shows in Paris, where fashion is taken very seriously, is a dream for every model. But it's also a gigantic amount of work, which Tyra understood, even at seventeen. Her mother, Carolyn, advised her, "If you want to be a model, you have to study hard. It's a job." So Tyra approached her modeling career with the same levelheadedness that she had applied to all other aspects of her life.

Tyra prepared for her trip by watching CNN's *Style*, with Elsa Klensch, and MTV's *House of Style*, with Cindy Crawford, over and over again. She particularly admired the way that Cindy had managed to parlay her career as a model into a more far-reaching industry and filed that information away for later!

Tyra also rented videotapes from the library of the Fashion Design Institute to learn how to walk correctly on the runway. In the beginning, Tyra says her model strut was lame, lame, lame. "My ankles would shake and I would bend my knees and stick my lips out," she joked to *People* magazine. And the first time she walked down the runway—a small one in Los Angeles—"I was horrible. I ⟨...⟩

stuck out 'cause I thought that was s⟨...⟩

In September 1991, she flew to ⟨...⟩
Tyra ever traveled without a chapero⟨...⟩
weeks, Tyra landed spots on the runwa⟨...⟩
shows—including those of legends Yv⟨...⟩
de La Renta, Chanel, Giorgio Armani, and Karl Lagerfeld.

It was an unprecedented feat for a newcomer and an especially impressive one for Tyra. Why? It turns out that Tyra didn't really fit the mold of a typical runway model. That "super-skinny" teenager was actually too curvy for a lot of the clothes. She told the *Sun-Sentinel* newspaper, "Since I was busty, they'd cut the clothes up the back to fit me. Mr. Armani would bind my chest. It was still a struggle because I was so voluptuous." In an industry where beauty tended to fit one particular standard, Tyra was successful not in spite of her unique looks, but maybe even because of them!

Her typical runway walk—a little more of an exuberant, animated bounce than other catwalkers'—also differed from the norm. "I created my own look and style; on the runway, I was the only one of the girls who didn't walk like a soldier." But it set Tyra apart in a positive way. "The first time I did his show, Todd Oldham told me to 'work it,' but he didn't know I would really 'work it.'" The crowd went crazy for her routine.

er catwalk style to some animal instinct. "She

of a gazelle. She was just born with grace."

Bethann Hardison, president of a management company for models (and former runway walker), raved about Tyra's walk to *Essence*. "She works the runway like the black beauties from the 1970s—the Pat Clevelands, the Alva Chins, the Billie Blairs. Or the black models you see in church fashion shows. Tyra knows her role on the runway: She entertains, but at the same time, she knows she's there to sell. And she does just that." Or as fellow supermodel Niki Taylor once described Tyra's signature moves, "That girl is a live wire. She can work a runway like you would not believe."

A promising career on the catwalk and commercial success—Tyra had it made, right?

Not so fast—there's always a price for success, which Tyra was soon to learn. . . .

Despite her initial success on the job, Tyra has often talked about how tough life was in Paris. She told *Details* magazine that the other models thought she was "antisocial and a [witch], but I didn't want to go to dinner with a lot of models, and all they would talk about was getting a rich man or how fat they are."

Tyra hardly behaved like the typical supermodel. In fact, she has never been much of a party animal. "I didn't drink, I didn't smoke, I didn't do drugs or anything like that in high school, so when I started modeling, I was just the same person."

That person didn't really feel at home in the Paris party scene. "I didn't speak the language, and I'm not very social. I tend to be myself, so I didn't have a lot of friends. I'd go to movies by myself. And I was pretty lonely, because a lot of models like to party and drink and hang out, and I wasn't into that."

Instead of attending wild parties, Tyra would hang out by herself. She mapped out the site of every Burger King, McDonald's, and Häagen-Dazs in the city of Paris and made sure to get her food fix at one of them every day.

Her mom sent her care packages of junk food. Of course, Mom thought Tyra indulged her sweet tooth occasionally, but for a time Tyra used the food as comfort. So she ate sandwich cookies for breakfast, peanut brittle for lunch, and caramel corn for dinner. She almost fainted on one runway because she was eating so poorly.

"I was very lonely," Tyra admitted. "I was depressed. I ate McDonald's and ice cream all the time. That's what I survived on."

But much like back in elementary school, where Tyra relied on her mother's comfort to endure the teasing of her peers, in Paris, Tyra also leaned on her mother to get by. She survived on daily phone calls with her mom, her biggest supporter. Eventually, Carolyn decided to quit her job and move to Paris and manage her daughter's career.

Chapter 3
Mother Knows Best

H ave you started to notice how much Tyra depends on her mom?

Tyra considers her mom to be her best friend in the world and says her mom's advice helps her get through all her tough times. Her mom also kept her levelheaded as Tyra's career started to take off.

"My mother told me not to believe the hype," boasted Tyra to the *Philadelphia Inquirer*. "These people aren't really loving Tyra. It's just the girl in the pictures that they are loving. Mom told me years ago, and I know that it's true, that the phone may be ringing today, but it can stop ringing tomorrow, and that has kept me grounded from the beginning." (For more about Tyra's amazing mom, see Chapter 17.)

Keeping Tyra grounded meant making sure she honed an incredible work ethic in Paris. She learned the importance of being punctual, professional, and poised. For that, she earned a reputation from fashion designers, makeup artists, and photographers of being down-to-earth instead of a diva. At a time when certain supermodels were becoming notoriously self-centered and difficult to work with, Tyra's attitude was all the more refreshing.

In the end, Tyra had Paris for only a year. She never did attend college but has talked about going someday. Instead, she majored in Supermodel.

Chapter 4
Tyra Breaks Through

*L*oneliness and language barriers weren't the only challenges that Tyra faced at the beginning of her career. She also found it incredibly challenging to be one of a few African American women trying to make it big in the modeling world.

For one thing, Tyra says it was harder for her than her white peers to find steady work. "There's not really a big representation of black models as compared to white models. So it is more difficult if a black model wants to get in the industry. As a white model, you have a lot of rejection. You add color to that, and it's ten times the rejection," Tyra explained.

Tyra did get good career advice from veterans like Beverly Johnson and Iman (who she simply calls "The Queen") but was disappointed to find little support from other models closer to her own age. She told the *Philadelphia Tribune*, "I got more support from divas in the past than divas in the present!

The only model who really kind of helped me along and was very sweet to me when I just started was Veronica Webb. . . . It just wasn't like this sisterhood when you first start and everybody comes and helps you."

Tyra has repeatedly mentioned the lack of camaraderie among black models in interviews—particularly the abuse she received from one when she first arrived on the scene. She admitted to *People* magazine, "I had a lot of problems with a particular model being very mean and just trying to ruin my career. I would go home and cry to my mom every single day on the phone."

On the whole, Tyra's been a class act and refrained from getting into a verbal catfight by naming the tyrant. But rumors have always circulated that the mean model was none other than Naomi Campbell. Campbell, a British-born supermodel, was discovered when she was fifteen, hanging out in London's Covent Garden. Until Tyra came along, she was the hottest black model in the world, receiving raves on the catwalk and a first-time cover for a black woman on French *Vogue*.

She also had a reputation for being a nightmare to work with. According to a fashion insider interviewed by *People* magazine, "She comes in two hours late and never apologizes. If there's another model there, you can forget it. She'll delay the shoot as long as possible because she doesn't want anyone else in the pictures." All of a sudden, Tyra appeared on the scene, and the fashion industry and media began to refer to her as "the new Naomi."

It didn't help matters that the comparison to Naomi was so favorable to Tyra. While Naomi was stubborn and spoiled, Tyra was agreeable and friendly. So it was no wonder that more and more work was getting funneled Tyra's way.

Naomi was furious and refused to speak to Tyra on several occasions. In March 1992, she reportedly threatened to bow out of Chanel's show if Karl Lagerfeld didn't bar Tyra from appearing on the runway.

Tyra has never specifically accused Naomi of bad behavior. She even corrected *Newsweek* when they ran the following comments and claimed Tyra said them about Naomi. "She did so many hateful things, like getting me thrown off shows because she was more famous." Banks said she never uttered Naomi's name to the reporter.

But Tyra does admit that the whole situation was very stressful for her.

"No model should have to endure what I went through at seventeen," said Tyra in *Essence* magazine. "It's very sad that the fashion business and press can't accept that there can be more than one reigning black supermodel at a time. People compared us everywhere I went, so there was constant tension between us.

"The industry kept touting me as the new Naomi Campbell. It was ridiculous, because I looked up to her before I started. It was like there's room for only one black model, so for me to be successful, I had to bring another one down. Naomi heard about it and just panicked," Tyra told *GQ*. (The two have since kissed and made up, with the help of Tyra's talk show. You can find out what exactly happened in chapter 14.)

Tyra understood these feelings of panic because she saw that there weren't a lot of opportunities for African American models in America. She said to *People* magazine in 1994, "I have twenty magazine covers in Europe and only a few in America—*Essence*, for one."

"Unfortunately, this business only embraces one African American beauty at a time," she has also said. Which meant that in order to succeed, Tyra would have to be doubly determined.

Luckily enough, that wasn't a problem for her.

Chapter 5
A New Attitude

*a*round this time, Tyra realized that she controlled her own attitude to tough times. Instead of giving up, she made the decision to be a woman who looks at things with an optimistic, glass-half-full philosophy.

Tyra always manages to find the positive in every aspect of her life.

About her awkward looks, she said to *Jet* magazine, "I've always been told by the fashion industry that if my forehead were an inch smaller, I would have been a little too plain-looking. Too pretty-girl-next-door-looking for them. The high forehead set me apart. In the black community, a big forehead is a negative thing. You hear that your whole life, but when you go into modeling, it's a positive thing. The modeling industry can instill a lot of insecurity in women, but at the same time, they find beauty in odd things. It can raise your self-esteem in some ways."

About the lack of true sisterhood and support in the modeling world, Tyra says, "It was hard, but it made me more independent. It made me find out things on my own." And about how tough it was to be a black model? That only made Tyra more determined than ever to succeed. Just a year after complaining about her career prospects to *People* magazine, she told *Essence* about her whole new attitude. "I've detached myself from the nonsense that goes along with being a black model in this business. I think things will change for the black models that come after us. They won't have to feel so insecure about losing their spots. They'll benefit from our pain."

And Tyra did go on to break down an awful lot of barriers for other African American models.

Chapter 6
Breaking Barriers

*a*fter nearly a year in Paris, Tyra returned to the United States in the fall of 1991. She felt incredibly excited and determined to make the transition from a high-fashion model to a highly commercial, household name.

Tyra has joked that the decision stemmed from a realistic re-appraisal of her body. Although she weighed about 140 pounds, certainly a healthy size for her five-foot, ten-and-a-half-inch height, she was much more voluptuous and curvy than the normal model. (Tyra candidly says the average model weighs closer to 120 pounds.) As she said to Diane Sawyer on *Good Morning America*, "I used to do *Vogue* and *Harper's Bazaar*. I was seventeen and skinny, but then I was twenty, and I got a little booty; you know, things were happening. And I was like, I'm not going to starve myself like I see my colleagues doing. I can't do this."

Good for Tyra! She would never deprive herself to fit one else's expectations. But she also knew she probably uldn't continue working the runways, either. "My body is changing, and seamstresses are calling me *grosso* in Italian, and I know what that means," she said.

Instead of giving up, Tyra decided to take charge. "I didn't want to be another model waiting for the phone to ring and hoping that Karl Lagerfeld, as much as I love him, would use me for his collection. I wanted to be in control of my career."

It didn't take long for Tyra to realize that there was another niche she could fill in modeling. She realized that no black model had succeeded in the commercial world before. "I've always been attracted to models whose careers tapped into the commercial, like Cindy Crawford and Claudia Schiffer. Like them, I have a little more meat on my bones. For runway and fashion magazines, they're always looking for the new thing, and they kick out the old ones. I just noticed that the commercial market hadn't been tapped by black woman before."

So Tyra forced her agent to query successful brands for work. And Tyra quickly started doing advertisements for some of them—including Liz Claiborne, Ralph Lauren, Swatch watches, and Pepsi. But she really struck gold when she became

only the third black woman to get a mul
represent a major cosmetics company. In 1
a Cover Girl.

It was a huge deal for Tyra. At the time
to look as lovely as the Cover Girls did. The print advertisements
and TV commercials, which depict girls talking about looking
"easy, breezy," were the epitome of American beauty. And
Tyra's wholesome girl-next-door sexiness couldn't have been a
more perfect fit. Just hearing Tyra talk about herself proved she
really was that innocent, wholesome girl in the commercials.
After all, this was the model that avoided the party scene in
Paris, instead choosing to be a homebody! "I went to work and
then I went home. A party for me was going to a movie that
was in English," Tyra told *People* magazine once.

Many of Tyra's friends actually tease her about her
homebody ways and call her an "old lady." But Tyra takes her
position as a role model seriously. When asked to talk about
her first sexual experience in *GQ*, Tyra refused: "I can't talk
about that. I'm a sweet 'Cover Girl.'" But there was already a
hint of sassiness accompanying her sweetness as she added,
"Cindy Crawford can talk about that sort of thing because
she's Revlon."

At this point, Tyra's career became one groundbreaking
accomplishment after another.

In 1996, *GQ* magazine crowned Tyra Woman of the —and put her on their cover. She became the first black woman and model to appear on the cover of *GQ*. It was one of their top-selling issues ever. Just one year later, she followed that feat with an even grander one. Tyra earned a spot on the cover of *Sports Illustrated*'s annual swimsuit issue.

The sports periodical features a bevy of beautiful models posing in bathing suits in gorgeous locales across the world every February. And each year, men swoon and women pledge to exercise more after seeing it on newsstands. In 1997, Tyra shared the cover with Valeria Mazza, a model from Argentina. It was the first time in thirty-one years that a black woman got the nod. Tyra felt pleased with the opportunity. But that didn't stop her from wondering out loud why the first black woman to get the cover had to share with a white woman. Fortunately, *SI* didn't hold a grudge about her outspoken comments.

Just one year later, the cover was all about Tyra, wearing a tiny pink-and-red polka-dot bikini. Elaine Farley, *SI*'s swimsuit editor, says the cover image, which was shot in the Bahamas after a previous one in Turkey hadn't satisfied the magazine, is one of the most memorable. "It's a dynamic shot. She's coming right at you."

And Tyra really did seem to be everywhere you looked around that time.

She made it to *People* magazine's 50 Most Beautiful list—two times. Tyra handled her success with typical self-deprecation, telling *People* that in reality, she's "just real goofy. I try lowering my voice and talking sexy—at least on my answering machine, but it just doesn't work." Two years later, when she earned the beauty nod again, she said, "I'm not ugly, but my beauty is a total creation. I'm not 'street-fine.' Street-fine girls are so drop-dead gorgeous, they make you gasp. I'm more model-fine."

You'd think all these accolades would be enough, but Tyra had one frontier in modeling to conquer—and she was even willing to lose just a little of the innocence to get it. In 1997, Tyra signed on to be the first black model to sell Victoria's Secret line of lingerie. And boy, did she sell it! Tyra graced the cover of their catalog in a leopard-print Nicole Miller swimsuit. It was so well received that the company chose Tyra—along with Heidi Klum, Rebecca Romijn, Adriana Lima, and Ines Rivero—to be their "angels" and promote their line of sheer bras and panties while wearing eight-foot-wide wings. The tagline? "Good angels go to heaven. Victoria's Secret angels go everywhere." How appropriate for the brand—and for Tyra.

In 1999, VS debuted a live fifteen-minute webcast of twenty models wearing their lingerie on a runway at a downtown Manhattan restaurant. The cybercast was the world's first virtual fashion show, and it nearly crashed Internet servers when more than 1.5 million people logged on to see the angels.

The Victoria's Secret Fashion Show enjoyed ratings success in a pre-Valentine's Day television spot. In 2001, however, it aired on ABC on November 15, the traditional pre-Christmas holiday slot. It was taped live in a tent in New York City's Bryant Park, the Angels flying over the crowd to the strains of a live gospel choir. This was the first-ever network broadcast of the annual event, and was billed as the "sexiest night on television." Other attempts to drum up hype included a performance by Italian tenor Andrea Bocelli, as well as a guest stint by the Angel models on a concurrent episode of *Spin City*. According the *Washington Post*, the show won big in ratings, scoring over 12 million viewers (slightly more than half of whom were female). And thus, an angelic tradition was born . . .

Tyra talks like a typical pro when asked about all this dizzying success. She told the *Philadelphia Tribune*, "I don't think I'm a trend. I'm a businesswoman. And the reason I have so many contracts and corporate advertisements is because I represent that if you put money in me, it's going to make money for you."

But she did more than make money for these

corporations—and for herself. She's reportedly worth $8.8 million.

Tyra did what she came to do. "I wanted to be the girl next door like Cindy Crawford, but I am a black model, and that meant I broke down a lot of doors. When I look at young black models today, I hope they can just walk through the doors like everyone else."

Chapter 7
Lights! Camera! Action!

*I*n just a few years, Tyra proved she had what it takes to be a huge success in the modeling world. Her looks and charisma made her a household name. Now it was time to figure out her next step. It can be difficult for any model to have longevity in his or her career. The business is always looking for the next big thing. For instance, Giselle Bündchen was discovered when she was only fourteen. But here, as always, Tyra's business sense was a huge help for her. She was savvy enough to understand a model's career can be short. Once again, her mom played an integral role in helping her.

Tyra told *Jet* magazine, "My mother told me never to believe the hype. Don't believe the hype because it's not real. They are in love with your product. Your product happens to be your physical self and a little bit of your personality too, but that's what they're after. When they don't want it anymore, don't feel discarded. Just know that your product isn't hot

anymore. Know that you'll have to revam[...]
into another field."

Tyra was still incredibly popular an[...] course, but in order to keep herself fresh and [...] listened to her mom's advice. She decided to [...] to her repertoire. Of course, Tyra had been interested in film long before she even considered modeling. Remember, she signed up to study film at Loyola Marymount before her stint in Paris changed her plans. "I wanted to be an actress, director, and producer long before I became a model," she reminded *Essence* magazine in 1995.

Anyone who saw Tyra on the runway knew the girl was a natural performer. "I think it's just something that comes naturally to me. I like acting the fool! I usually act the fool with my friends. In fact, when my mom's friends used to come over for the holidays, I'd get my cousins and friends together. We'd choreograph dances and songs, and I'd always be the lead singer and perform. So I just have that inside me."

She also always comes prepared. Tyra says the best career advice she ever got was, "Study your craft. If you want to be a model, learn every photographer and makeup artist. If you want to act, get your butt into acting class."

Tyra's first actual role was a bit part—playing a supermodel in *Inferno*, a one-hour British television movie. Talk casting! Tyra and fellow models Kate Moss, Helena stensen, and Eva Herzigova play scantily clad women who keep disturbing an English author from finishing writing his book in southern Italy.

Tyra's real break came in 1994, when she earned a recurring role as Jackie Ames, Will Smith's sassy romantic interest on the popular NBC show *The Fresh Prince of Bel-Air*. On it, Will Smith played a teenage boy who leaves his family in Philadelphia and moves to California to live with rich relatives. Tyra impressed the producers when she showed up for the audition already in the character of a college student, wearing a T-shirt and sneakers. She explained to them that she loved to watch the fish-out-of-water sitcom, which was another point in her favor. She proved to be a good match for the six-foot two Smith. (Ironically, Smith's real-life wife, Jada Pinkett Smith, didn't get a part on the show four years earlier because producers thought she was too short—Jada is five feet tall—to be a romantic match for Smith.)

Tyra played Jackie Ames for seven episodes. "Boy, it was a trip working with Will," Tyra said. "I remember it was hard to get through a scene without laughing until I cried." Tyra's part was a popular one, and producers wanted her to stick around, but she already had other plans. "I loved *The Fresh Prince of Bel-Air* for half a season, but then everybody started coming up to me on the street and calling me Jackie Ames. I felt like I didn't want to get stereotyped into that character."

Lucky for Tyra, she could afford to wait for the right roles. "My modeling career gives me the chance to make a lot of money and not have to worry about acting to eat and to live. So I act when I want to or when I find something that's fun or interesting for me to do."

Although Tyra knew she wanted to act, she tried to be careful about the roles she picked. She even declined the chance to appear as the woman who seduces Tom Cruise one night on the beach in the Cayman Islands in the hit 1993 legal thriller *The Firm* because she thought the part was too one-dimensional. "I don't want roles that scream, I AM SO PRETTY."

More than anything, Tyra wanted to be funny on-screen. "I look up to people like Jim Carrey, and they make me want to show the comedy talent I have—the physical comedy. I think that'll surprise people. They'll say, 'Oh, my gosh, she can do that!' I want to show people all the different sides of me."

While waiting for just the right role to come along, acclaimed director John Singleton spotted Tyra on the cover of *Essence* magazine in June 1993 and decided she would be ideal for a role in his next film. It wasn't the comedic role Tyra had been hoping for, but it offered something else.

Little did Tyra know that in addition to making her major movie debut, she would also lose her heart and enjoy her first serious romance.

Chapter 8
Young Love

Tyra continued to search for just the right role to launch her movie career. Instead of a comedy, her film debut turned out to be heavy drama about racial tensions. The film, *Higher Learning*, also introduced Tyra to celebrity romance when she met and began dating John Singleton, the film's director.

In 1991, John Singleton seemingly came out of nowhere when he wrote and directed his first film, *Boyz N the Hood*. The low-budget film about a boy attempting to resist the temptation of crime and drugs in South Central LA went on to win two Oscar nominations—for best director and best screenplay—and bestow on Singleton the reputation as the next big thing in the film world. (He was the youngest ever and first African American to get the directing nomination.)

Singleton grew up in the tough South Central LA neighborhood he chronicled in his movie. He split time between the homes of his parents—Sheila Ward, a pharmaceutical salesperson, and Danny Singleton, a financial planner, who had separated from Sheila when John was young.

Just like Tyra, John went to the movies one day and left with a dream. He knew he wanted to be a filmmaker ever since he saw *Star Wars* at the age of nine. ("I was overwhelmed. I knew I wanted to make films when I left the theater.") Unlike Tyra, John remained in Los Angeles and attended UCLA's prestigious film school.

John caught a glimpse of Tyra in *Essence* magazine and wanted to cast her in his third film. So in the spring of 1993, mutual friends introduced John to Tyra, and, not a big surprise, he was smitten with the model from the get-go. "When I saw her on the runway, it was, '[Wow], she is beautiful.' I was dying," he told *People* magazine.

Although Tyra was very attracted to John, she wanted to take the relationship slowly. After all, she was only nineteen. When John first told her he'd like their relationship to be exclusive, Tyra put him off because she "didn't want to rush things." But later, during a romantic stroll in Manhattan, Tyra realized she was madly in love and devoted to making their relationship work. "In front of the Empire State Building, I told him I wanted to be his girl," Tyra confessed in an interview the couple gave to *People* magazine about two years into their relationship.

The couple became inseparable, even with separate successful careers as a jet-setting model and Hollywood it boy that made finding time together difficult. That actually strengthened their bond for a while. John explained this attraction to *Ebony* once. "She is a good girl and very smart. She has a lot going for her. I want a woman who's got a mind. Tyra helps me out a lot. She helps me unwind. It's a real crazy business, and it helps to have somebody who understands how difficult it is."

Tyra can be outspoken about many things, but she's always been pretty guarded about the men in her life. Her comment about John was much more succinct than his. "I like that he's very intelligent but not nerdy."

Tyra also loves romance. And John made a point of demonstrating his love in a big way. During their relationship, he lavished Tyra with gifts. He threw her a surprise birthday on a chartered yacht for her twentieth birthday. A year later, he one-upped himself by giving his girlfriend a beautiful sapphire-and-diamond friendship ring.

Those were the advantages of dating each other. Making things slightly difficult—other than their hectic careers—was Tyra's youth and their different backgrounds. Tyra was only nineteen when she met the twenty-four-year-old. And though they had grown up only twelve miles apart from each other in Los Angeles, their lives were quite different. Tyra's middle-class life and finishing-school pedigree didn't much resemble John's tough-guy childhood. As Singleton teased in the *People* interview, "She never waited no tables. I worked my a— off my whole life."

John was willing to give his girlfriend a job, provided she worked for it. Although he spoke highly of Tyra's acting on *The Fresh Prince of Bel-Air*, offering the praise, "She adds flavor to what could have been a throwaway role," he did make his girlfriend audition for her part in *Higher Learning*.

According to Singleton, his film is based on his own experiences while attending UCLA as a film major. The film deals with students' growing awareness of the major racial and sexual differences between them.

Tyra knew the part of Deja, the love interest of the main character, was a strong one for an actress just starting her career, but she also worried about what everyone else would think of Singleton casting his girl. Having to audition for Deja (the character was named after John's Siamese cat) made it okay. According to *Entertainment Weekly*, Tyra let everyone know how things stood. "John said, 'Read for it, but if you're bad, you don't get it. I'd look like I'm thinking with my you-know-what.'"

But Tyra impressed the producers yet again and got

the part! The film also stars Laurence Fishburne as a college professor, Omar Epps as Banks's fellow track star and love interest, and Oscar winner Jennifer Connelly as a lesbian activist.

Tyra told *Entertainment Weekly* that she took the part for two reasons. "It's not glamorous, and I liked it that John made her smarter than the guy."

Tyra's part is small but pivotal. And she does have some intense lines. "I feel like fighting," her character says about the discrimination minorities face on campus. "It's a waste of time. Instead, I fight with this," she says, pointing to her head.

The fledgling actress approached her job with the same amount of preparation that she did the catwalk.

Tyra trained for her role as a college track star by working out with Jeanette Bodin, the head women's track coach at UCLA (and an Olympic gold medalist!). Tyra has described the training as her "biggest athletic challenge to date." In just three short weeks, she learned how to hurdle. Track was never a sport she participated in growing up, so she had to learn everything from scratch. She worked out for four hours a day, seven days a week.

All the hard work paid off, and Tyra received rave reviews for her intense performance.

In the end, she enjoyed working for her boyfriend.

"Being my first movie, it was nice that it was somebody directing it who loved me. So he directed me with love," Tyra gushed to CBS when the film hit theaters.

What wasn't as easy for the two of them was Tyra's love scene with co-star Omar Epps. "That was really hard. It was the second day of production. Me and Omar didn't know each other at all, so we had to kiss, and like, you know—it was weird. But we got through it." Not Singleton—he told *People* that "it was the hardest thing for me."

The couple dated for two years, but they never lived together because Tyra says she's just "old-fashioned" that way.

Alas, like many cases of young love, Tyra and John didn't last. While they both remained mum about the specific cause of their breakup after two years, Tyra's age may have had something to do with it. When asked about future marriage plans, John always said, "We're too young for it right now. Tyra's definitely too young."

And while Tyra continued to act in movies and several television episodes, she found her higher calling elsewhere.

Chapter 9
Model Role Model

*I*f you think Tyra was content with all her modeling gigs and acting nods, you don't know Tyra by now. The self-described workaholic was already on the lookout for her next challenge.

She told the *Miami Herald*, "The beginning of my modeling career was all about myself. It was how many covers can I get, or how many doors can I knock down—because so many people were telling me as a black model I wouldn't be able to accomplish certain things and I wouldn't be successful in the fashion industry—so it was all about me, me, me, me!"

But once she'd proved people wrong, Tyra knew her next step had to be doing something for others. "Now it's about helping other girls. It's so important to give back," Tyra told *Parade* magazine.

Tyra has always felt that it's important to make a positive difference in other people's lives if you can. In 1992 (quite early in her career), Tyra used the first flush of her fortune to create a scholarship for African American girls at Immaculate Heart, her high school alma mater in Los Angeles. Each year, she pays for the tuition of one financially disadvantaged student. "I was very privileged that my mother and father sent me to private school. I want other African American girls who can't afford it to experience that kind of education." (Tina Gardner, the first recipient of the Tyra Banks Scholarship, excelled at the school, even becoming junior class president.)

After that contribution, Tyra looked around for a charity she could support. In 1997, she became a spokeswoman for the Center for Children & Families. The nonprofit organization offers safe houses and counseling for disadvantaged children and their families in New York City. It provides everything from housing to food to literacy classes and drug treatment.

Tyra's initial involvement with the group was to judge a finger-painting contest for their Cards from the Heart series. She chose six winners—not an easy decision since there were well over sixty pictures—but all for a good cause. Sales of the greeting cards help fund Kids Success, a tutoring program for kids who read well below their grade level. When Tyra lived part-time in New City, she visited Kids Success classes as often as possible. "They seem shocked when I remember their names and ask them about problems they mentioned before.

It's nice to know I can touch them personally," Tyra explained to *InStyle*.

In 1997, Tyra was honored by the Starlight Children's Foundation for her efforts to help kids. Tyra was thrilled to receive their Friendship Award but already understood the real prize. "What these kids do for my heart is what I really cherish. It really is true what people say: When we volunteer our time and talents to help others, we're the ones who truly benefit."

It was a simple statement, but it marked yet another new chapter in Tyra's career—and her life: Tyra as role model.

Chapter 10
Tyra's Literary Turn

*S*oon enough, Tyra found that interacting with kids was amazingly rewarding. She wanted to do even more. She realized that young girls looked up to her as a role model, and she wanted to live up to their expectations.

Each year, Tyra receives thousands of letters from fans. Much of the mail asks for her tips on makeup, clothes, exercise, and boys. But a lot of it also thanks Tyra for being just a little more approachable and realistic than many of the other models in the world. After reading the fan mail, Tyra knew she had something special to share. What better way for Tyra to give back than to help girls realize that everyone—even a glamorous supermodel—goes through insecurity at some point in their lives?

Tyra began by speaking out about her own experiences with low self-esteem. She gave speeches at summer camps and women's summits. She even got the opportunity to talk about the subject at some prestigious universities, including Howard, Georgetown, and Johns Hopkins.

These speeches helped give Tyra the idea of writing a book that would share her beauty and fitness tips but would also give girls tools for building their self-confidence.

And with the help of Vanessa Thomas Bush, a writer for magazines like *Glamour*, *Swing*, and *Life*, Tyra went through her old journals and photo albums and asked experts in the fields of beauty, fashion, fitness, and health for their unbeatable advice. The result is *Tyra's Beauty Inside and Out* (HarperCollins). Tyra's personal essays about subjects serious (getting a friend to open up about emotional abuse she was suffering) and silly (getting grounded by her mom for dyeing her hair jet black) are intermixed with smart and simple tips for looking your best. It's straight talk about health and fitness, love (there's advice on whether to take a platonic relationship to a romantic level), and makeup (pencil eyeliners work better than liquid or felt-tip ones).

In fact, the book had such frank advice on some subjects—like sex—that one unnamed chain store refused to sell it on its shelves. Tyra didn't mind the snub, though. "That means I'm doing my job," she said.

Sure, there were some people who thought, *What does Tyra really know about having to boost one's self-confidence?* In fact, in 1997, a young woman in the audience during Tyra's lecture at Georgetown University asked her, "Why do you come here to speak to us about self-esteem when you have every reason to feel good about yourself? Not every woman can look like you do." Tyra calmly tried to explain that she was simply sharing her tale—and being honest about her own past experiences. She writes in the book, "I know some people may still say they don't want to listen to someone whose life seems to be so full of glamour, where everything is handed to her on a silver platter. If you think that, take a look at some of the photos."

Yup, Tyra included photos from all stages of her life—the awkward to the awesome.

One photo shows Tyra untouched, "to give people a better idea of the kind of magic makeup artists work." It shows Tyra with zits, puffy eyes, and dark circles and even a slight mustache shadow. Sure, in the last few years, it's more commonplace to be up front about all the retouching that happens in Hollywood, but Tyra was real enough to reveal it ages ago.

(This trend toward being "natural" was something that Tyra would continue to explore as her career evolved; she has appeared on her own talk show and in several magazines unretouched or not made up—which is very unusual and very brave in this day and age!)

Tyra, who dedicated her book to "the women before me who paved the way, to Daddy who paid the way, and Ma who paced the way," may have lost that image of perfection, but she found her voice in this book.

She writes, "I've learned the most important things in life—staying true to your beliefs, forming close friendships, developing an independent mind, being fit and healthy, and most of all learning to love yourself."

The book was a huge turning point for Tyra. Although she continued modeling and acting for a while, she seemed to find her calling. All along, Tyra had said she didn't want to be "perceived as a brainless beauty." There was no chance of that now! *Now* she had a plan!

yra loved the experience of writing the book *Tyra's Beauty Inside and Out* so much that she decided to be even more proactive in her efforts to help young girls struggle with self-esteem issues. She had obviously hit a nerve because she continued to receive thousands of letters and e-mails from young girls, thanking her for sharing her tales of self-doubt.

Tyra had found her cause. Not only did Tyra have the financial ability to help others now that she was one of the highest-paid supermodels in the world, she also realized that she could truly empathize with these girls who were trying to grapple with body image and boy problems. Why Tyra? She's just one of those lucky few who finds it easy to talk to just about anyone. She revealed that skill to a *USA Today* reporter— "I've always been what people call approachable; on the street, people are like, 'You're cool and you weigh twenty pounds more than those other girls in the Victoria's Secret catalog.

And you're funny and crazy.'"

In 1999, Tyra and her mom started TZone, a leadership program for disadvantaged teen girls from four high schools in the Los Angeles area. Their mission statement: to provide a fun and supportive program that reinforces core values of trust and support, challenges teen girls to resist negative social pressures, and enhances self-empowerment—inspiring girls to become confident leaders in their communities.

The following summer, the first TZone camp opened in the Big Bear Mountains, near Santa Barbara, California. Tyra wanted her nonprofit foundation to run a camp because of her fond memories of attending one when she was younger. "I have great memories of camp—just having the camaraderie of girls that weren't from the same background thrown together. That's what happens at my camp," she said.

Tyra reads every application and personally chooses the girls who will attend. The camp is free, and priority is given to girls from low-income backgrounds. Each summer, TZone selects sixty girls, age thirteen or fourteen, enrolled in a ninth-grade class.

Since its inception, 240 girls have thrived from their weeklong stay at Camp TZone, where they participate in activities designed to help them get motivated, develop leadership qualities, and realize their personal goals—and personal power! There are also late-night sing-alongs to enjoy.

And Tyra is with the campers every step of the way. "I'm like a big sister to them. I'm a friend and a mentor." She even runs some of the group talks. In an interview with the *Sun-Sentinel*, she spoke about what happens at TZone. "We do a lot of sharing and crying. And the girls are allowed to have a private session with me if they want. I told everyone when we started this thing that I was not going to just put my name on something and not be involved. This is important to me. I am there for the girls. I choose everything. I even choose each and every menu. It's important to me that everything be perfect for the girls."

Tyra insists on that because of her immense desire to make a difference in kids' lives. "I've always loved kids. I think that if I had chosen another job, it would be in education. I really try to have a lot of fun with the girls. I tell them I don't have all the answers. I don't tell them how to live. I'm no therapist." (Because of TZone, though, Tyra is now a trained crisis counselor.)

Instead, Tyra uses her inner goofball to help. "Basically, I use humor. Like this one girl who was very skinny was telling me how all the kids tease, grabbing her arms and saying, 'I can fit my whole hand around your entire arm.' I told her I went through the very same thing. So she and I decided to run it around with some funny comebacks. We would practice. I would come up to her all week and pretend to make fun of her and she would use her comebacks. Later, she told me that she wasn't scared of the first day of school anymore."

Tyra admits that the girls are a little intimidated in the presence of a real-live supermodel in the beginning—"The first day, I see they're kind of staring and asking to take a picture with me. After a while, I'm doing the rope course with them or leading the talks. . . . Girls are coming up to me every single day, going, I thought you were going to come here in an evening gown with a tiara on a golf cart and be waving to us, and, 'Oh, thank you, and it's so nice to see you,' on the last day. They didn't know I was going to be here every single day. I stand up there and I cry with them, and it just shows them that there is humanity in everybody and that everybody has insecurities. No matter how successful I am, no matter how big I get, I'm still the insecure skinny eleven-year-old. Yes, I was very lucky, but I take the responsibility to give back and show we're all going through the same thing."

In short, they may all look at Tyra as "The Supermodel" when they arrive, but they end up calling her by her camp nickname—that would be BBQ—at TZone.

Tyra still has major plans for TZone. She hopes to open TZone camps around the country soon. "But I want quality control," she said to the AP wire service. "I want it to be like McDonald's or Coca-Cola. It's the same everywhere."

She's also in the process of transforming the foundation into a year-round initiative that would operate quarterly summit meetings and community service programs. What's key to the TZone team is that the organization increase opportunities for TZoners to volunteer all-year round, not just participate for that one week.

Tyra proudly tells people that the foundation is the most exhausting work she's ever done. "It's harder than any acting or fashion shoot I've ever done. I slept fourteen hours straight after the camp session ended."

Chapter 12
Ties to Oprah

By 1999, Tyra Banks had earned a reputation as an outspoken, openhearted African American woman who talked about her incredible life experiences in a relatable, "you go, girlfriend" style. She also demonstrated a huge desire—and ability—to make a difference in girls' lives.

Does this sound like any other media dynamo you know?

Oprah Winfrey has simply become a legend for her amazing efforts to make the world a better place. In 1997, she spearheaded a spectacular charitable endeavor. What began as a campaign to get viewers to (1) donate their spare change for 150 scholarships for the Boys & Girls Clubs of America and (2) volunteer their time and energy to help build two hundred homes for Habitat for Humanity turned into Oprah's Angel Network. The organization has raised a staggering $27 million to help fund worthy causes around the world, in part because

Oprah pays 100 percent of the administrative costs to ensure that all the money goes to charity.

But before she made such a contribution to philanthropy, Oprah started with a talk show on ABC twenty years ago. Since then, *The Oprah Winfrey Show* has been a ratings bonanza and its hostess has become arguably the biggest cultural influence on television today.

Few things in life are certain. One of them is, if Oprah is on your side, you're golden!

Just think of the number of individuals whose careers have been made by Oprah's support. When Oprah touted Rosie Daley, her personal chef, and Bob Greene, her fitness trainer, for their help with her amazing weight loss, their expertise became highly in demand. Both went on to write best-selling books—*In the Kitchen with Rosie* and *Get with the Program*.

Oprah has had an amazing impact on America's literacy as well. She founded her very own book club in an effort to get people reading—and it's paid off! Oprah has turned unknown literary writers—like Chris Bohjalian and Jacquelyn Mitchard—into regular *New York Times* best-selling authors by choosing their work for her book club. Even Dr. Phil, a psychologist who got Oprah's attention when he counseled her during a libel trial, is now a star in his own right, with his very own show.

More recently, Oprah has introduced the public to

interior designer/decorator Nate Berkus and cookbook author and television food guru Rachael Ray on her talk show. Now Nate's merchandise is sold at Linens 'n Things around the country and Rachael is about to star in her very own talk show, produced by Oprah's production company.

It's practically down to a science. If you're a favorite individual of Oprah's, you're going to succeed.

Imagine Tyra's thrill when Oprah Winfrey personally requested that Tyra join her talk show as a monthly youth correspondent in 1999.

Tyra found her two-year stint on the show to be valuable television experience. It wasn't acting. Instead, it was all her real personality.

Just being in the presence of Oprah taught Tyra so much about the direction she wanted to take her career. Oprah is one of Tyra's idols. "Even though she is one of the richest women in the world, she is the 'realest,' most down-to-earth person you'd ever want to meet," raves Tyra. "Everyone can relate to her, which is a wonderful quality to have." (Check out some of Tyra's other favorite women starting on page 110.)

Tyra recognized what makes Oprah so influential and explained the secret to her success in *Fortune* magazine: "The biggest thing about Oprah is her authenticity. She is so true. There is no pretense to her, and the audience knows it."

According to the folks at Warner Brothers, when Tyra appeared on the show, Oprah's ratings were 8 to 10 percent higher than for other episodes. The other regular guest who enjoyed such good ratings? Dr. Phil. Now he's a household name, too.

Many people thought that Oprah's hiring Tyra meant she planned to hand over the reins of her talk show to Tyra. (That's probably not going to happen anytime soon. Oprah recently renewed her contract to stay with the show through 2008.)

Even if she doesn't take over Oprah's spot on the show, Tyra is eager to follow in her footsteps. Tyra has often said she envisions herself as a Gen-X Oprah. "I want to be successful across the board. I want an empire like Oprah's. I may do it with a little more cleavage, but I plan to get there."

And she's certainly on her way. In the fall of 2005, Tyra got her very own talk show.

But we're getting ahead of this particular Cinderella story. First, there's the matter of a little show called *America's Next Top Model*.

Chapter 13
Tyra Takes on Reality TV

*T*yra is a total TV fiend. Some of her favorite shows include *Will & Grace*, *Curb Your Enthusiasm*, and *Commander in Chief*.

And she can't get enough of reality TV, even *Being Bobby Brown*. ("Come on! It's so hard not to watch," Tyra writes on her website.) She's a huge fan of MTV's *The Real World* and *American Idol*. She has one complaint about *Idol*, though. She wishes she could see more behind-the-scenes segments on the singers' lives after they leave the stage.

One morning, while Tyra was hanging out in the kitchen in her underwear making her morning tea, the words *America's top model* popped into her head. Suddenly, Tyra had the notion to meld *American Idol* and *The Real World* into one show about the highly competitive world of high-fashion modeling. "I wanted to do a show where people were striving for a goal, winning something [they] worked hard for." A TV show about what it really takes to make it in the profession would be a great way to answer the question she was constantly asked by strangers when they met her: "'How do I become a model?'" Tyra joked to the *Washington Post*, "There are so many people coming up to me and asking how to get into the modeling business. I thought, 'How can I get all these people off my back?'"

Confident that her idea was something the public would watch, Tyra quickly passed it to her agent. Her agent was dubious, but UPN president Dawn Ostroff wasn't skeptical at all. She bought the show in a matter of hours.

In the spring of 2003, the competition for *America's Next Top Model* began. By now, everyone knows the premise of the show. A large casting call—just like the one on *American Idol*—takes place, and the judges winnow a thousand girls down to a small group (it was ten competitors during season one, but now there are twelve to fourteen each time).

The girls move in together, and the camera follows them around for eight weeks as they endure a boot camp of sorts for models. (Like *The Real World*, their residence is fabulous! One year, it was a Manhattan penthouse in the historic Waldorf-Astoria hotel.) The wannabes have to endure tough challenges that actually take place in the real cutthroat world of high fashion. They've had to look sexy while being photographed underwater, look happy while posing in bikinis in the bitter cold, and look calm while being photographed with a tarantula crawling across their bodies.

Tyra and her regular team of beauty experts work with the girls to hone their craft. Jay Manuel, a sharp-tongued makeup artist and photo director, helps them prep for photo shoots. And J. Alexander teaches them how to walk the runway. (He also judges them on their performance.) Tyra's around to dispense advice or chide them for their mistakes.

Viewers tune in to see how the girls fare and whether they'll be any catfights, but there's no question that the elimination scenes are appointment TV.

At the end of each episode, the panel of judges from the modeling world—including Miss Tyra—eliminates the weakest link in the group. The girls are rated on their modeling style, physical fitness, photo shoot adaptability, and publicity skills. The elimination process can be as trying to watch as the tribal meetings on *Survivor*.

The judges in the original season included *Marie Claire* fashion editor Beau Quillian, fashion designer Kimora Lee Simmons, and former supermodel Janice Dickinson. Dickinson made headlines for her caustic and blunt commentary. She's even made *American Idol*'s Simon Cowell appear tame!

Tyra's take on Janice? "Bless her heart, I hired her, but

she does have a very opinionated and strong way of speaking to the girls . . . and all of it doesn't get on camera. I'm in that editing bay going, 'I think that one's a little bit too strong. We're not gonna use that.'" She adds, "Janice will make a statement that the girls can do nothing about. Like, 'Your feet are too big! I hate big feet!' What can someone do about that? Then I'll say, 'So you've got a size eleven. Turn them this way— they'll look like a size nine.' That's the way I critique the girls. But we love to hate Janice."

In season five, Tyra replaced Dickinson with sixties supermodel Twiggy. "Janice is an amazing woman—a handful, but amazing—and gives the best sound bites in the world. But we mutually decided that she should start doing other things. Twiggy is nice because she's a mama figure."

Simmons and Quillian also left, and more recent judges include Nigel Barker, a former model and photographer; Nole Marin, a fashion editor and stylist; and the show's own "Miss" J. Alexander.

The winner of *America's Next Top Model* receives representation with a modeling agency, a contract with a cosmetic company (like Revlon or Cover Girl), plus a spread in a fashion magazine (*Marie Claire*, *Jane*, and *Elle* have all done the honors in the past).

Along with co-executive producer Ken Mok, Tyra runs

the show. She is heavily involved in every aspect. In 2004, she told *The Early Show*, "People think I just show up at work and do the on-camera stuff and leave. But I'm hiring directors, balancing the budgets, choosing locations. All the photo shoot ideas come from me and my team. And I'm editing thousands and thousands of hours of stuff every single day."

She e-mails her staff in the middle of the night with ideas. And she's willing to do manual labor if that's what is needed. She even hot-glued beads to the set of the show at 3 a.m. to make a deadline.

And Tyra wouldn't really want it any other way, although she swears she's going to start delegating someday. But for now, Tyra tells *The Early Show*, "I am such a control freak and such a perfectionist, every single frame of that show, every music cue, the lighting, I am so involved in."

Tyra confesses that she would never have lasted on her show if she had to compete. "I always say that if I tried out for *America's Next Top Model* when I first started modeling, I wouldn't have made it. Physically, I would have been fine, but personality-wise, I would have felt like I was in front of college admissions people and that I had to say the right answer."

But the only right answer, insists Tyra, is to be yourself. "Stop being fake. I need you to be real. What works is being real and just being very open."

Being real has been the key to Tyra's success all along, and she's happy to share that secret.

America's Next Top Model has also given Tyra the chance to try and change a few things she has found wrong with the industry. Tyra demands that the contestants be a diverse group. ("Who is going to connect with ten skinny blondes on TV? I wanted women of all colors, ranging from skinny to full-bodied—the idea was for women to see reflections of themselves.") And she screams whenever anyone gives the girls too hard a time about their bodies. Sure, Tyra understands the realities of modeling, but she's not going to let anyone mess with those girls' minds when it comes to their body image.

The show has become so successful, it helped put the fledgling TV station UPN on the map. (Don't worry—it's also been renewed for two more competitions even though UPN just merged with WB to form CW.) In its fifth season, *ANTM* was number one in its time slot among women ages eighteen to thirty-four! And season six began in March 2006.

What excites Tyra even more than ratings, though, is the opportunity to be a creative force. She told *Sports Illustrated* that she had never felt so satisfied with her work up until *ANTM*. "It's been really stressful. My stomach aches, and I haven't had a manicure in months, but it's something I've always wanted to do. It's nice to finally be in charge."

Chapter 14
Trying a Talk Show

*T*yra finally got the chance to have even more control—and pressure!—when she agreed to host her own talk show. For five years, the folks at Telepictures tried to get Tyra to commit to a talk show. They believed she had all the right moves to succeed in that format.

Executive Jim Paratore described Tyra's appeal: "She has a feel for this generation of women. . . . There're not a lot of people like Tyra who have the ability to cross over from topics with real people . . . and then also sit down and feel comfortable with a celebrity. . . . When you look at her, she defies expectations. She's a very relatable, open person. And she's a hands-on producer. She will be the driver of this show."

Another executive, Dick Robertson, even uttered the comparison that was on everyone's minds—"Like Dr. Phil, Tyra has cut her teeth with *Oprah*. She's extremely smart, very grounded, and also easy on the eyes. We think she's got the talk show goods to pull this off. . . . Tyra is a very impressive person; she's obviously more than a model. It's her appearances on *Oprah* that we looked at and said, 'If ever there's a future Oprah, she could be the one.'"

How amazing is that? Not only does Tyra get to work for her idol, she's told she has what it takes to literally follow in her idol's footsteps.

Tyra downplays the comparison whenever she can. "The next Oprah! Damn, I don't compare! I lost a lot of sleep about that early on," Tyra fretted to *Fortune* magazine. "Oprah has been an incredible success for twenty years and I'm just starting."

When Telepictures approached Tyra years ago, she didn't feel ready for the challenge. Her main concern was she didn't have the life lessons necessary to command people's attention and offer them guidance. "At twenty-five, I hadn't experienced a damn thing. But going through negative experiences and bad relationships truly prepared me." And she noticed a void. There wasn't a talk show hosted by a member of Generation X.

Tyra turned to two TV veterans, Oprah Winfrey and Jay Leno, for advice. Former employer Oprah told her to go for it. "She told me people are going to feel like they know you because you're on TV every single day. This is a whole different life, so get ready for it. She's been really helpful."

Tyra also asked late-night host Jay Leno for some words of wisdom. "He has given me so much personal advice on how to be a great talk show host. Jay told me to be myself and to listen to my instincts and to remember that people love to laugh. He has told me that you can find humor in even the saddest situations and that sometimes laughter is the best medicine."

With encouragement from those two pros, Tyra focused on making her show her own. She showed up on day one with more than 180 ideas. The show is aimed at women between ages twenty-five and thirty-five, but Tyra stresses that all ages are invited. What's most important to Tyra is that it's a place where women can face their demons or find their inspiration. Tyra defined her goals for the show to *Fortune*. "It's not really a talk show. It's a woman's guide to life. It's topical, connected to the news, but we do fashion and fun stuff. It's like different pages or sections in a women's magazine. They're unique, but they all fit together under one cover."

The Tyra Banks Show shares Oprah's interest in discussing issues that really matter to women. "I wanted to create a place where a woman of any age could hear inspiring, enlightening, and moving stories that really speak to them.

I hope it gives women the feeling that they have a support system—to help them deal with life. That's an empowering feeling," Tyra explains.

Tyra is aware that it's an uphill battle and many other personalities have failed with their own talk shows. But she's still game. "I'm very aware of the odds against any new talk show making it on TV. I want to find out my quirks, my strengths and weaknesses. I want to have a show that people haven't seen before," exclaimed Tyra to *Parade* magazine.

While finishing post-production on the fifth edition of *America's Next Top Model*, Tyra taped episodes of her talk show. She was her biggest critic.

"I'll tape a show, and I'm a perfectionist—I'll look at it backward and forward. I see that when I don't trust my instincts, I don't feel right looking at it."

The show debuted on September 12, 2005. In a nod to her past career, guests make their appearance on the show by walking down a runway. Tyra chose to have one because it represents her mission to empower people. "The runway symbolizes something in society that's kind of intimidating." That is, until one walks down Tyra's runway. "The reason I wanted a runway onstage is that I feel like it's an intimidating thing for most people. I wanted to spin that and make it an empowering place so that women on my stage—once they've accomplished something or expressed themselves—they can get up on that runway and celebrate it." And it's working. "They have so much fun, they don't want to get off."

The harshest comments about the show have been that Tyra is using her platform to revisit past issues and working them to her favor.

Case in point: In one of the earliest shows, Tyra had a sonogram to finally put to rest rumors that her voluptuousness comes courtesy of plastic surgery. "I'm tired of this rumor. It's something that's followed me forever." (For the record, Dr. Garth Fisher, a plastic surgeon from ABC's *Extreme Makeover*, concluded that Tyra's 34C bust is natural. She also made the men in the audience leave the room while she was tested.)

For November sweeps, Tyra invited model Naomi Campbell to the show to reconcile after all the past tension between them. But it wasn't for revenge. Tyra told New York's *Daily News*, "I wanted to do this show because sisterhood is so important to me. I feel like women hate on each other—we're jealous—and it has to stop."

One of the highest-profile episodes so far had Tyra wearing a fat suit to experience how society treats obese people. She came up with the idea after having breakfast with some friends. "There was every race at the table, gay and straight, but when the subject of obesity came up, my friends started talking in a rude way." So in October 2005, Tyra climbed into a prosthetic suit that added two hundred pounds to her frame and walked around a popular neighborhood in Los Angeles. "It was one of the most heartbreaking days of my life. I started walking down the street and within ten seconds, a trio of people looked at me, snickered, and started laughing in my face. I had no idea it was that blatant."

She hopes that show will make people think twice before teasing someone for being overweight. "I hope this show will cut down on the cruelty."

Oprah would be proud. And Tyra is on her way to achieving her latest goal. "I wanna be the voice of my generation with my talk show."

Chapter 15
Turning in Her Wings

*B*eing the voice of a generation takes an awful lot of energy. In 2005, Tyra decided it was time to say goodbye to her modeling career so she could focus on *America's Next Top Model,* her daily talk show, and the rest of her life.

She had never planned to model as long as she did. "When I was eighteen in Milan, they were asking me about my dreams and goals, and I said, 'I'm going to retire from modeling when I'm twenty-three or twenty-four and have my own talk show!' Okay, I was wrong on the age part."

Of course, Tyra—at the ancient-for-a-model age of thirty-two—left in high style. Her fitting farewell took place on the Victoria's Secret runway on Tuesday, December 6, in a red lace bra and underwear with a belt made of military medallions. The medallions might as well represent all of the battles Tyra had fought and won along the way. She had faced down rejection, cruelty, and competition—as well as her own nagging insecurities.

Tyra couldn't contain her joy as she spoke to the throngs of reporters who had come to cover her swan song. "I'm not just retiring from the runway; I'm retiring from all modeling. God, I love saying that! When I was eighteen, my mom said I had to have a plan. I decided I'd leave on top. I want to be like athletes who seem stuck in time. When you see them at fifty, you say they can probably still run like a champ."

The other Victoria's Secret models working that night—including Giselle Bündchen, Naomi Campbell, and Heidi Klum—convinced the company to let Tyra take her angel wings home with her. What a farewell gift! "It's really a big deal because you never get to take the wings home because Victoria's Secret loves to display them in museums."

Tyra joked that retiring also granted her some final power. For the first time ever, she got to choose what she wore for her final stroll down the runway. In addition to the red lace, Tyra cavorted in a black satin corset and an embellished push-up bra with a beaded organza cape adorned with feathers. "I chose my three favorites. I've never had that clout before. Retiring is good."

So what will Tyra do next?

She's already achieved a lot in just thirty-two years.

She succeeded as a model on her own terms. Mind you, what made the difference was Tyra's attitude, her unwillingness to give up. As she says about her earlier misfortune, "I'd go home and cry a little bit and pick my butt right back up and go in there again."

She then went on to demystify that world of modeling for the rest of us and conquered reality TV in the process.

She's trying to inspire a generation of young girls to get over their insecurities and self-doubts and make the best of their lives. And she's got her very own talk show.

So, seriously, what's left for her to do?

Ken Mok, Tyra's co-executive producer on *America's Next Top Model*, predicts power.

"In five years, she will have a media empire. I'm not kidding. She has in her head a whole game plan of being a media mogul."

And Tyra says she's already planning to produce a sitcom, a one-hour drama, and two television movies.

She's also looking a little more inward herself these days, reassessing her belief that career success happens without romantic success. "I used to tell my mom, 'I think I traded it off,' and she'd say, 'If you think that way, then you probably did.' I'm not living in that fear that I'll never find love anymore.

I want to get married. I want to have kids. But you've got to time it right. There's a way I could do that now."

Her social game might still need a little work, though. As Tyra will tell you, "I have a seventy-year-old woman's social life and a fifteen-year-old girl's energy."

But given her success with everything else she's tackled, we're sure this dynamo will soon figure this out as well!

Chapter 16
Tyra's Men

Long before it became an unwritten rule for celebrities to try and not reveal too much about their love lives, Tyra chose to be coy about her romantic status. "I won't say if I'm single or dating or married or divorced. There are boundaries," she has told interviewers.

Sure, she's willing to speak honestly about the feelings we all go through when it comes to love. In her 1998 book, she opened up about the subject. "Lord knows I've had my share of love woes. I don't know how many of you have said the words 'I love you,' but I think I've uttered them more than once too often. . . . Since I first started dating, I've had only three boyfriends, and all of them left me heartbroken and crying on my mother's shoulder."

On her talk show, she said her ideal man is "a guy who's my age, who has a good job and can take me out."

But from the likes of her former beaus, it appears that

Tyra also likes her men to be as accomplished as she is, no matter what their profession. Check out the bios of the few celebrities who stole Tyra's heart—at least for a short time.

Tyra
Banks

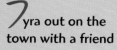

$\mathcal{T}$yra steps out with
Tom Jones and
Stephanie Seymour.

$\mathcal{T}$yra out on the
town with a friend

$\mathcal{O}$n the set of
The Tyra Banks Show

*T*yra walks the runway
on her talk show.

*W*ith the judging panel on
America's Next Top Model

Totally
**more than just
a pretty face!**

John Singleton
Film Director

Dated Tyra from 1993 to 1995

Singleton was born on January 5, 1968, in Los Angeles, California. He was the youngest director—and first African American one—to receive an Oscar nomination for directing. The film in question, *Boyz N the Hood*, was his film debut. He also received a screenwriting nomination for it. Singleton went on to direct *Poetic Justice, Higher Learning, Baby Boy, 2 Fast 2 Furious*, and *Four Brothers*. In 2005, he produced the critically acclaimed film *Hustle & Flow*.

Isn't it romantic? When asked to name the most romantic thing anyone's ever done for her, Tyra said John Singleton once decorated her house with candles to welcome her home from Paris. "He gave me a bath and dried me off. I walked downstairs, and there was a chef and a table laid out with all my favorite foods. For dessert, there was a big basket of perfectly cut watermelon. I really love watermelon. Of course, I started crying."

Current romantic status: Singleton had a short-lived marriage to actress-screenwriter Akosua Busia. They have a daughter, Hadar. Singleton also has a daughter, Cleopatra, from a previous relationship.

Seal
Singer

Dated Tyra in 1996

Seal was born on February 19, 1963, in Paddington, England. The soul and R&B singer coped with a penniless childhood in London and a bout with lupus when he was young. The Grammy-nominated singer is best known for the songs "Crazy" and "A Kiss from a Rose."

Isn't it romantic? Seal's breakup with Tyra provided some of the emotional inspiration for his 1998 album Human Being, including a heartfelt plea for forgiveness in "When a Man Is Wrong."

Current romantic status: In 2005, Seal married German supermodel Heidi Klum (one of Tyra's friends and fellow Victoria's Secret angel) on a Mexican beach in May 1995. Their son, Henry, was born on September 12, 2005. They're also raising Leni, Heidi's daughter from a previous relationship with an Italian businessman.

Chris Webber
Pro Basketball Player

Dated Tyra from 2002 to 2004

Chris Webber was born on March 1, 1973, in Detroit, Michigan. He was the 1990-91 National High School Player of the Year. During his rookie year in the NBA, playing for the Sacramento Kings with a $123 million contract, he was the first rookie to total more than 1,000 points, 500 rebounds, 250 assists, 150 blocks, and 75 steals, which helped him become the 1994 Schick NBA rookie of the year. He currently plays forward for the Philadelphia 76ers.

Isn't it romantic? While on vacation in Maui, Hawaii, in 2002, Chris and Tyra dined at Sarento's on the Beach one night and took a walk in the sand while the restaurant's staff placed a bottle of Cristal champagne, at Webber's request, on their table. When they returned from their stroll, Tyra had tears in her eyes and a ring on the third finger of her left hand. (Still, their publicists always denied they had gotten engaged and, two years later, announced the couple had broken up in July 2004.)

Current romantic status: Single.

And while we're on the subject, contrary to what you may have heard, Tyra has strongly denied ever dating the following celebrities: Michael Jordan, Tiger Woods, Kobe Bryant, Rick Fox, and Mark Messier. "Those guys are great, but nothing ever went on between us."

And Tyra's advice to the brokenhearted? Find a new hobby!

As Tyra herself says, "Whenever I feel sorry for myself when my heart's been broken, I try to take all that energy I would have wasted moaning and crying and direct it into something positive. I've come away with some great hobbies because of this. After [one] breakup, I took up painting pottery. Now I have all these personal creations, from ceramic bowls to salt and pepper shakers, that I made to decorate my home and those of my close friends."

Talk about making lemonade out of lemons! But Tyra's positive attitude isn't surprising to those who know her.

Chapter 17
Mother Knows Best, Part 2

Of all the wonderful women Tyra finds inspirational, no one matters to her as much as her mom, Carolyn.

Carolyn London-Johnson, a native of Los Angeles, married Tyra's dad, Donald, in 1972. After seven years of marriage, London and Banks divorced when Tyra was six and her brother, Devin, was eleven. Carolyn is now married to Clifford Johnson, a high school graphic arts teacher. The remarriage was a tough adjustment for Tyra. "I remember feeling like someone had kicked me in the stomach. I felt betrayed. She was going to let this man take her away." Eventually, Tyra and Clifford bonded, and she says without his discipline and influence, she wouldn't be able to clean a house, cook a meal, and iron clothes better than most of her peers.

Carolyn also ran a strict household but an open one. Tyra wasn't allowed to wear makeup out of the house until she was thirteen, but she always could talk to her mother about any serious subject. "She is so brutally honest with me. I've never had to experiment with any type of drugs or get involved with any type of sex early because I can ask my momma anything," Tyra raved to *Women's Wear Daily*. "I'd ask, 'Momma, what's crack?' And she'd answer, 'Well, crack is this, the pipe looks like this, let's open up the crack dictionary.' That bluntness and that realness allowed me to survive in this industry full of insecurity."

Before she became Tyra's manager, Carolyn worked in the field of biological photography. For fifteen years, she was employed by renowned California teaching hospitals like Cedars-Sinai and the Hospital of the Good Samaritan. In 1989, she developed her own home-based glamour portrait business.

Carolyn felt some early trepidation about daughter's foray into the unknown world of modeling. "I let [Tyra] go, but I was terrified. I didn't sleep. I cried. She cried. From the beginning, she knew I didn't want her to go. She had a choice of going to college or going over there, and I let her know the decision had to be hers and that I would support her however I could," Carolyn recalled to the *Philadelphia Inquirer*.

Eventually, that support led Carolyn to quit her job as a manager of the photography laboratory at the Jet Propulsion Laboratory and follow her daughter to Paris. "I went to Paris because [Tyra's modeling agency] was very concerned about [Tyra's] success happening so rapidly. They wanted me to come there so they could school me about the industry, and although I had a full-time job, I took a vacation and went."

Carolyn paid close attention and learned much about the business of modeling. When Tyra begged her to manage her career, she went for it. "I quit my job, and it was the scariest thing I have ever done, but it was the best thing I could have done. It gave her the freedom to concentrate on her work. I learned very quickly that the fashion industry is very fickle and that the models have very little control over their careers. They come and go, and only a handful transcends every trend. We wanted that control, so we hired a publicist to let the public know who Tyra really is and what she is about. We said let's direct this to John Q. Public."

Carolyn is the main supplier of valuable advice to Tyra about living life. She's the reason her daughter never gives up, always has a plan, prepares diligently for every goal she has, and tries to help others in the world.

Tyra credits her desire to help others to her mom. "I take after my mom. She's always the one who guides the girls in my family through things."

Perhaps Carolyn's best piece of advice, though, is what lets Tyra be Tyra. "You cannot 'fake the funk,' as my mom says.

You have to be yourself, and it has to come from a true place. People will either embrace that or not, but at least you didn't try to be something else and then fail and go, 'Oh, I should have been myself!'"

Tyra's taken that advice, and look how far it's gotten her. (Carolyn's wise counsel is available to everyone now. Just log on to Tyra's website and go to the "Ask Mama" section. Carolyn will answer your questions.)

Fortunately for Carolyn, Tyra knows the importance of giving back to those who've helped you in life. She's reciprocated in a few amazing ways.

In July 2001, Tyra arranged for her mom to get a makeover, care of *The Oprah Winfrey Show*. As Tyra said on the show, the more famous she got, the more her mom focused on Tyra's rising stardom instead of herself. "The more successful I got, the more she started going into a shell and just putting everything into me and my brother. And she just took a backseat. My mom is in a rut. She always wears sweats. Her life is me and my brother and her granddaughter, and she's just forgotten about herself."

Once Oprah's show got ahold of her, Carolyn was treated to a brand-new look, including a hair weave.

Finally, Tyra moved her mom into a five-thousand-square-foot, five-bedroom Mediterranean-style house in

Beverly Hills. She originally bought it for herself, "but it was too big, so I gave it to my mother."

Chapter 18
Tyra's Filmography

Thanks to her fierce work ethic, Tyra has a lengthy list of film credits to her name! Rent a bunch, invite some friends over, and have yourself a totally Tyra movie slumber party!

Higher Learning
1995

The cast: Omar Epps, Jennifer Connelly, Kristy Swanson, Regina King, Michael Rappaport, and Laurence Fishburne.

The plot: A drama about racial tensions developing among students at a fictitious college campus.

Tyra's role: Deja, a brainy track star, in love with a fellow athlete, Malik (Epps).

Fun fact: Singleton originally cast Tupac Shakur in Epps's role and Leonardo DiCaprio in Rappaport's place. Both had to drop out. DiCaprio had a scheduling conflict, and Shakur was sent to jail!

Love Stinks
1999

The cast: French Stewart, Bill Bellamy, and Bridgette Wilson.

The plot: A struggling sitcom writer finally scores a date with his dream girl. Only problem: She turns out to be a nightmare.

Tyra's role: Holly Garnett, the best friend of Chelsea, the psychotic beauty.

Fun fact : Bridgette Wilson (Chelsea) is actually happily married to retired tennis sensation Pete Sampras.

Coyote Ugly
2000

The cast: Maria Bello, Piper Perabo, Bridget Moynihan, and Adam Garcia.

The plot: A sexy comedy about an aspiring songwriter who comes of age while working at a bar full of wild women.

Tyra's role: Zoe, the former bartender/dancer turned law student, who introduces Violet, the main character, to Coyote Ugly, the bar.

Fun Fact: Jessica Simpson auditioned for the lead character but dropped out because of the sex scenes. Eventually, those scenes were cut from the finished film anyway.

Love and Basketball
2000

The cast: Omar Epps, Sanaa Lathan.
The plot: A romantic drama about two aspiring basketball players—and next-door neighbors—who spar on and off the court while falling in love.
Tyra's role: Kyra Kressler, the woman who briefly comes between the couple.
Fun fact: In real life, lead actress Sanaa Lathan played basketball as poorly as Tyra did. A WNBA coach finally had to teach Lathan some key moves on a basketball court.

Life-Size (sure, it's technically a made-for-TV movie, but it co-stars a virtually unknown Lindsay Lohan, so we couldn't resist)
2000

The cast: Lindsay Lohan, Jere Burns.
The plot: A doll comes to life and helps a family reconnect after a tragic loss.
Tyra's role: Eve, the doll, who works magic.
Fun fact: The producers wanted Daryl Hannah for Tyra's part, but she turned them down.

Eight Crazy Nights
2002

The cast: The voices of Adam Sandler, Kevin Nealon, Rob Schneider.
The plot: An animated musical comedy about Davey Stone, a thirty-three-year-old slacker who gets in trouble with the law and has to referee a youth basketball league as part of his community service.
Tyra's role: The voice of a Victoria's Secret gown.
Fun fact: Sandler's real-life wife, Jackie Titone, voices the love interest.

Halloween Resurrection
2002

The cast: Busta Rhymes, Sean Patrick Thomas, Jamie Lee Curtis.
The plot: Legendary serial killer Michael Meyers is back for the eighth time when a group of college students spend the night in his childhood home as part of a "reality" Internet contest. Mayhem and carnage ensue.
Tyra's role: Nora Winston, the assistant to the slick man behind the contest.
Fun Fact: If you look closely in the scenes of Jamie Lee Curtis's character at the sanatorium, you see a photograph of hottie Josh Hartnett. Why? He played her son in an earlier Halloween movie.

Chapter 19
One False Note

Only one project of Tyra's hasn't been a huge success. In 2003, Tyra wanted very much to venture into the world of pop music. During the second season of *America's Next Top Model*, Tyra took a risk and debuted her singing voice in a video that aired on the reality show. "I've been singing for six years. I've been in and out of studios with top producers, but it wasn't something I was ready to express to the public or the press."

She enlisted the help of some top talent in the music industry, including songwriter Diane Warren and producer Rodney Jenkins. Jenkins, who had worked with the likes of Janet Jackson and Mariah Carey, told *Jet* magazine, "People will be really shocked. She can really sing. She's like between a soprano and high alto. She has what it takes to pull this off. Some people want to be divas in the studio and work for three or four hours."

Tyra even harbored fantasies of releasing an album. "I have five songs that I really love. I've done tons of them, but I think five are album-ready now."

She was smart enough to know it wouldn't be easy. "You only get one chance when it comes to the music world. You might do a movie. It flops. You get another chance. With music, this song has to be hot."

Alas, there are no plans to let the public hear Tyra sing anymore. The single didn't exactly fly up the music charts.

But Tyra even laughs that disappointment off. "[Forget] being a singer. I wanna be the voice of my generation with my talk show."

Chapter 20
She Shoots, She Scores!
Tyra and Basketball

ave you noticed how often the subject of basketball has played a part in the story of Tyra Banks's life?

Here are ten tip-offs to why it's Tyra's favorite sport.

* Tyra used to bond with her dad by attending Lakers games when she was a child.

* Basketball is the sport that highlighted her body image. Tyra was tall enough to get picked for the team but uncoordinated enough to never really get the chance to play.

Her first big acting role? Tyra plays a college student on a basketball scholarship in *The Fresh Prince of Bel-Air*.

 When Tyra gets the solo nod on the cover of the *Sports Illustrated* swimsuit issue, the magazine profiles her while visiting the Lakers in the locker room on game night. (She even moisturizes Shaquille O'Neal's arms!)

 Okay, she doesn't get to play ball herself, but the best-reviewed film in Tyra's resumé is called *Love and Basketball*.

 Eight Crazy Nights, another one of Tyra's films, centers around a youth basketball league.

 LA Laker star Kobe Bryant recorded a hip-hop album, although it was never released. One single did get some radio airplay. The song, "K.O.B.E.," was a duet with Tyra.

One of Tyra's most high-profile relationships was with Chris Webber, when he played forward for the Sacramento Kings.

 Tyra's website lists the people who have influenced her. At the top of the list? She gives accolades to former b-ball star and current Knicks team executive "Uncle" Isaiah Thomas. "He watches over me and makes sure I'm okay. He told me it's okay to be scared when starting new ventures."

 The last man that gossip columnists linked romantically to Miss Tyra? Giancarlo Marcaccini. Surprise! He was a well-known basketball player in Italy. Now he's in charge of a company that makes ice cream. (Smart man—that's another one of Tyra's loves.)

Chapter 21
Famous Last Words

By this point, you are well aware that Tyra Banks is nothing if not outspoken! In her quest to achieve so many successes, including serving as a role model to young women everywhere, Tyra has come up with some very memorable quotes. Below, find some of our favorites!

Tyra on Body Image

Despite all the attention Tyra receives for her beauty, she still vividly remembers how awkward and insecure she felt during her adolescence. For that reason, she always has a lot to say about society's effect on individuals' body image and sense of beauty. Here are some comments Tyra has made to the media about the issue.

"A lot of models become insecure because they feel that no one really appreciates their inner beauty. I've made sure that I've surrounded myself with

people to help me keep things in perspective. They remind me that all of the glamorous makeup, outrageous hairdos, fancy outfits, and rigorous sit-ups are just a means to an end: feeling good about yourself."

"We are judged by how we look; it's part of human nature. But that's only half of it. Without the inner beauty that comes from a strong sense of self, all we've got is a nicely wrapped package with nothing filling it."

On plastic surgery: "Totally against it. A lot of people think I have breast implants because I have the biggest boobs in the business. But I was a 34C in twelfth grade and a 34C when I first started doing fashion shows. In fact, there's a picture of me when I was seventeen years old on the runway in Paris. I have on a sheer top: huge, big, I'm still a C."

"I'm very interested in talking about body image—it's a Catch-22 with me. As a fashion model, I put out an image that's very difficult for young girls to live up to, but at the same time, I understand the psychology behind it and what makes a woman feel the way she feels when she looks at a [fashion] magazine."

"My silhouette looks fine, but I have dimples in the backs of my thighs. At the Victoria's Secret fashion shows, you will never see me walking with my drawers and bra on without a little skirt or drape in the back. I know where I got it. I'm not going to walk on a runway and show it."

"When I was really skinny, I hated my arms, so I always wore long sleeves——and to this day, if I'm on a date with a guy, I cover them up because I feel like he's staring at my arms. And they're not even super-skinny now!"

"All the black kids in school used to call me all kinds of horrible names. Then when I went to a mixed junior high school, all of my white friends would be like, 'Oh my God, you're so gorgeous. You're so skinny.' By the way, I looked disgusting. I looked sick. But they'd be like, 'You're so skinny. I wish I could be like you.' And all my black friends would be like, 'Girl, eat a pork chop! You are so skinny.'"

"I was taught at an early age that physical beauty isn't all it's cracked up to be and that pretty faces come a dime a dozen. We are in our bodies for life, so we should make the most of them by taking a positive approach to how we look and feel."

"I don't starve and I don't deprive myself. I eat some of everything I like, but maybe just not as much of it as I'd like to. That, combined with regular exercise, keeps me in pretty good shape."

"We always want what we don't have—longer legs, higher cheekbones, a flatter stomach, smoother skin."

"My body is a contradiction of proportion. I have a full bust and wide hips, compared to my thin legs and arms. I take that into consideration when I shop. You won't see me in a pair of white stretch pants because I have some cellulite, which I know isn't necessarily a horrible thing. It's natural and a lot of women have it."

"I don't think of myself as a diva. I'm too dorky! I don't want to be 'working.' I don't want to have to put on that 'thing.' I call it 'the thing' when I have to do my hair, pull on the lashes, get dressed up. When I go out for potato chips, I just want to go out looking like myself, which means you'll see bad pictures of me. It's just a part of life."

"A beautiful smile is truly one of our greatest natural resources. With one upturned grin, our face lights up and lets our inner light shine!"

Tyra on Men and Dating

While Tyra prefers to remain mum about the specific men she has dated in her life, she's always game to make good comments about men and dating in general.

FIRST KISS

"We were seeing Biloxi Blues at the Beverly Center. The guy kept trying to [kiss me], and I was like, 'What are you doing?' When we left the theater, I walked thirty feet in front of him."

TYRA'S CELEBRITY CRUSH

"Laurence Fishburne. He's sexy because he's intimidating."

TYRA'S TAKE ON GUYS WHO ONLY DATE MODELS

"I call them model groupies. In the late eighties, it was rock groups. These days, it's business types. I think it's kinda sad. I dated one and didn't realize until it was over. I'd be on jobs and the other girls would be like, 'Oh, yeah, I dated him, too.' Or you'd be around the house and see a framed picture of a model you thought was cut out of a magazine, but you find out it's a snapshot. So I've been there, and it makes you feel like a number, actually. It's about a man feeling like nothing without a beautiful girl on his arm. And you know what's really hard? When you date a modelizer you get insecure, because you don't want them to see you not looking like a model."

KISSING

"I've never even kissed a guy on a first date. Or held hands. I have these rules. Even on a third date, it's just going to be a kiss on the cheek. I'm not fast with that stuff."

DATING NON-CELEBRITIES

"I went out with a guy that didn't have a job. He had nothing. I flew him to New York. It was fun. I felt like the man. But it's hard to date a guy without money because a lot of them can't handle it. But it's funny—the guys that I've dated that have more money than me can't handle it either."

"Some guys are real slick and you can't tell what their agenda is. That's something that just takes a little bit of time. That's the kind of guy who will be really cool in the beginning, and then after a while, he's like, 'Dress up like you did in that picture and come with me to my high school reunion.' Or other times guys may show it off really soon in the beginning. They might just keep calling me by my full name a lot. You know, 'Tyra Banks, can you pass the salt?' Stuff like that."

ADVICE FOR DATING A MODEL

"Don't tell her that she's beautiful when you see her at work, because then she thinks you're talking to the model. Tell her when she comes out of the shower. Don't get too serious too fast, because then she'll think you're a model groupie if you're trying to hold on too hard. Bake something when you meet her parents

that shows you're normal and not some rock star or
actor. Once you get her parents, you'll get her."

THE KIND OF MEN SHE DATES
"African American brothers, in every shade they come."

WHAT TYRA WANTS
*"Just if they're really nice, really funny. Joke with me.
Don't be afraid to compliment me. A lot of guys think,
'Oh, you're a model, so I'm not gonna say you're
beautiful. I'm not gonna say your hair looks nice.' It's okay
to say that, because if a guy says that, it's different than a
photographer or a fan saying it. And just be aggressive!"*

BEING SINGLE
*"The older I get, the more I understand that it's okay to
be single. But I'm not going to say it's easy, especially in
such a couple-conscious world. From birth, women are
raised to hope for a Prince Charming to waltz us down
the wedding aisle. So to make that fairy tale come true,
we make it our mission to find that perfect partner, and
when we don't, we feel like failures. Well, I'm here to
tell you that there is life without a man. Fortunately,
I have a group of friends I can count on who help me
through times when I'm feeling down about the dating
scene. They've taught me there's a big difference
between being alone and being lonely."*

THE FEAR FACTOR

"Guys are afraid to date me. Even if I approach them and we go out a couple of times, they're comfortable in the beginning and then they, like, flip out. Because then they [realize] I'm normal and natural, acting all stupid and goofy and picking my nose and all kinds of stuff, and they're just like, 'Oh, you are so cool.' And they're like, 'It's a model! It's Tyra Banks!' And then they flip out and run away."

"A lot of men aren't strong enough to handle beautiful women. Then when somebody asks you out and they get a little aggressive—but in a smart way, you know, he's like flirting and paying you some attention—you're like, wow, I'll go out with you."

Tyra on Modeling

While the media may have fixated on Tyra's cleavage, cat-fights with Naomi Campbell, and alleged trysts with famous athletes, Tyra swears the topic she's most often asked about by real people is the modeling industry. Here's a compilation of comments Tyra has made about the profession.

"There's a lot more to being a model than looking beautiful. It's 20 percent fun, 80 percent hard work."

"I'm very blessed to be a certain height and to be born a certain way. At the same time, it is not who I am, it's what I do. I realize that [modeling] creates this image that's hard to live up to. It's important for me to let young girls know how much of it is smoke and mirrors."

"When I first started modeling, I wasn't the gorgeous girl. I had a big forehead and a narrow chin; my eyes are really big and far apart. But I guess that's what agencies are attracted to. We get beauty-queen-pageant girls come in, but they're a dime a dozen. That's not what necessarily makes a top model. It's the imperfection."

"I don't do nudity-nudity, but I will do very sexy shots. Sex sells, and modeling is very close to that slogan. You have to be open to that."

"Even when I'm fifty and no longer modeling, everyone will still refer to me as 'Tyra, the model.' Once a model, always a model."

"If you want to be a model you have to have very thick skin, because no matter how famous you get, you are still constantly being critiqued."

"The modeling industry goes in and out of different styles and body types that are supposed to be hot at that moment. But right now, the models are looking a little bit healthier to me, not like that heroin-chic thing. And when I say healthy, I don't even mean body type. I mean just facial pigment and stuff like that. They have blush on their cheeks again, and they look a little healthier. But still, such a stick skinny ideal, it would have worked for me when I was eleven years old because I was ninety-eight pounds and my same height. So I was really thin and insecure. It would have worked well for me to look at that in a magazine and see that was called beautiful. But the majority of little girls aren't that way. The majority of them are struggling with their weight. So I think it's important to show different body types and say they are all beautiful. Which is not really what they do. They tend to dictate a certain look every five to ten years."

"Black models don't make a lot of money in the fashion world because in order to make real money, you have to have the advertising."

"It isn't that simple, but you normally start by having a head shot and a full-body shot done and talking to a respected modeling agency. A lot of women are taken for thousands of dollars by crock agencies promising superstardom for a few thousand dollars. But stardom isn't something that can be bought and paid for."

"My years in the business have taught me that the camera doesn't lie. If I have a pimple, dark spot, or rough patch, it will definitely show up in a photograph. And while it's true that photographers do use retouching to erase noticeable blemishes, too much retouching can become expensive. That's why advertisers prefer to hire models with skin as flawless as possible."

"Who can blame teenage girls for fantasizing about modeling? It beats working at a yogurt stand."

"There's no shortage of beautiful faces entering the modeling industry on a daily basis. But for all the hundreds who walk through those agency doors, there are so many giving up and returning home. It's true: Beauty is only skin deep. The modeling industry is competitive, and many of the girls are extremely insecure. They worry about their weight, their public images, their looks, and the next hot young model that might take their place. If you don't have a strong sense of who you are and where you come from, the crazy modeling world will eat you alive."

"No woman should feel insecure when she looks at a model in a magazine. Nobody has any idea how much work goes into this."

"The only type of diva that is [acceptable] to me is somebody who's fierce, somebody who can command a crowd, and somebody who can make someone buy a magazine cover just by the look in their eyes. [But] that's where the diva stops. In terms of attitudes and demanding things and being difficult, that is not acceptable."

"The first thing you have to be is photogenic and connect to the camera. Connecting to the camera means connecting to the person looking at that magazine cover or at that ad. To be a top model, you have to have personality, you have to be able to do interviews."

"I think you have to have a combination of accessibility where everyone in America can feel like they know you. You need a certain sense of beauty, a beauty that's not too intimidating, where it doesn't scare people. You need a personality that's fun. You should be a person who can speak well and represent products."

Tyra's Favorite Women

This may come as a shock to readers, but Tyra has been as influenced by other groundbreaking women as young girls are by her! In her 1998 book, *Tyra's Beauty Inside and Out*, Tyra gave a shout-out to some phenomenal woman (including her idol Oprah Winfrey) she admires. You already read about Oprah in these pages, but check out these women to understand what impresses Tyra. Here's what she had to say about them, plus an update on what they're up to now.

Gloria Estefan

Singer (and arguably the most successful Latin crossover in pop music)

What Tyra said then: "Not only is she an incredible vocalist, but she also went through a terrible accident and made a remarkable recovery, all the while staying strong and never losing faith."

Gloria has recently released a DVD, *Live & Unwrapped*, that she recorded in Las Vegas at Caesars Palace. She earned her first producer credit on it. She's also written a children's book called *The Magically Mysterious Adventures of Noelle the Bulldog*. Gloria is married to Emilio Estefan, a music producer, and the mother to son Nayib and daughter Emily.

Vanessa Williams
Singer/Actress

What Tyra said then: "Full of strength and perseverance, she proved that everyone who doubted her was dead wrong. Success is always the best revenge."

After overcoming controversy as the first defrocked Miss America, Vanessa went on to make six hit albums and two gigantic songs ("Save the Best for Last" and "Colors of the Wind"). She's raising four children (son Devin and daughters Jillian, Melanie, and Sasha) from her two past marriages. Vanessa is currently starring in *South Beach*, a TV show produced by Jennifer Lopez (another female on Tyra's it list), and ready to release her next album, *Everlasting Love*.

Cindy Crawford
Supermodel

What Tyra said then: "She was the first to make everyone understand that modeling is a business, and for that she is one of the most respected women in the industry."

Currently, Cindy is raising her two children, son Presley and daughter Kaia from her second marriage to nightclub owner Rande Gerber. She occasionally returns to commercial work.

Maya Angelou
Author
(I Know Why the Caged Bird Sings)

What Tyra said then: "Her writing transcends all races, all boundaries, and touches everyone. No one who reads her powerful words can walk away untouched."

Currently, she is a Professor of Humanities at Princeton University.

Chelsea Clinton
Daughter of Former
President Bill Clinton and
Senator Hillary Clinton

What Tyra said then: "Even though she is the president's daughter, she is definitely her own person. And she does an excellent job staying as normal as possible while her life is being documented everywhere."

Chelsea is a business analyst on a public health care project for McKinsey & Company, a prestigious consulting firm.

Barbra Streisand
Singer/Actress/Film Director

What Tyra said then: "People tend to put women down who show strength and know what they want, but those are the traits I admire in her."

Last summer, Barbra released the twenty-fifth anniversary edition of *Guilty*, her hit album with Barry Gibb.

Margaret Cho
Korean American Comedian (best known for a popular off-Broadway show called *I'm the One I Want* and a short-lived sitcom, *All-American Girl*)

What Tyra said then: "Her brand of comedy is strictly take-no-prisoners. She's not afraid to say what's on her mind, plus she's just downright funny."

Margaret's recent book, *I Have Chosen to Stay and Fight*, a compilation of humorous essays, was published in October 2005.

Toni Morrison
Author
(Song of Solomon, Beloved)

What Tyra said then: "She writes with such strength and beauty that it is easy to see why her work won the Nobel Prize for Literature."

Currently, Toni teaches Humanities at Princeton University.

Jennifer Lopez
Singer/Actress/Fashion Designer

What Tyra said then: "A very talented actress, she is making her mark in film by choosing compelling roles that give greater exposure to Latin cultures."

Currently, Jennifer is filming *El Cantante*, a movie with her husband, Marc Anthony, and concentrating on her successful clothing and perfume lines.

Kristi Yamaguchi
Olympic Gold Medalist
Ice Skater

What Tyra said then: "Although ice skating has lost some of its luster in the past few years, she is one of the few Olympic champions to retain the grace and beauty of the sport."

Kristi launched her own foundation, Always Dream, to help disadvantaged communities. She and her husband, professional ice hockey player Bret Hedican, have two daughters, Emma and Keara.

Terry McMillan
Author
(Waiting to Exhale, How Stella Got Her Groove Back)

What Tyra said then: "She broadened the audience for black literature and got people who had never opened a book to read."

Terry's most recent book is *The Interruption of Everything*.

Cheryl Miller
Basketball Star

What Tyra said then: "Back in the day, my dad took me to a USC basketball game where she was the star athlete. She opened doors for women in basketball. Because she was so tall and thin, she was also a good role model for me as I struggled with my body image. Now she's the coach of the WNBA's Phoenix Mercury."

Cheryl is a sports commentator for ESPN, ABC, TNT, and TBS.

Jackie Joyner-Kersee
Track Star

What Tyra said then: "She has asthma, yet learned how to work through that to become the best athlete in the world."

Jackie currently runs a foundation to help deserving individuals in St. Louis, her hometown.

Kerrie Strug
Gymnast

What Tyra said then: "Her courageous act to help the U.S. Gymnastics Team win the gold medal, even when she was in incredible pain (after stumbling through the end of her routine), was one of the most unforgettable moments of the 1996 Summer Olympics."

What women do you admire most? Compile a list and write down exactly what impresses you about them. It's a great way to focus on the things that matter to you—and figure out some of your dreams and goals. From this list, you can tell that Tyra places a lot of importance on overcoming adversity and trying different careers.

Chapter 22
A Fierce Fire Sign!

yra Banks is one fierce girl, so it makes sense that she has one fierce star sign—Sagittarius, to be exact, a fire sign. Fire signs are all about freedom, and they cannot be contained easily. Fire signs are known for their boundless energy, excitement, ideas, and joy. When it comes to a fire sign like Sagittarius, it's best just to hold on and enjoy the ride, because there is no stopping someone like Tyra once she gets started.

Sagittarius is the most energetic of the fire signs. Sagittarians are super-enthusiastic and love to take risks. They are open, adventurous, creative, fun, funny, impulsive, kind, idealistic, and independent—and Tyra fits that definition to a T. She is a fiery, spunky girl who loves to have fun and embraces life on the go. Sagittarians are known for their generosity and down-to-earth natures, which is probably why Tyra is considered the girl-next-door of the modeling business—she's just too nice and humble to ever be considered pretentious or a diva.

Tyra is a typical Sagittarius in that she adores traveling and is always brimming with new ideas and projects. Her sign's boundless energy helps Tyra keep up her hectic schedule while still giving everything she's got to every project that comes her way. Occasionally, all that enthusiasm and involvement can be a drawback if a Sagittarian spreads herself too thin, but luckily, Tyra has her family and friends to keep her from pushing herself too hard. Family is very important to Sagittarius, and they are fiercely loyal and affectionate when it comes to those dearest to them, which is clear to anyone who has seen Tyra and her mother together!

One of the biggest weaknesses of a Sagittarius, and one that Tyra has miraculously turned into a positive, is their restlessness and need for constant change and travel. Tyra has embraced this side of her nature and uses her ever-evolving career and travels throughout the world to feed her desire for change and excitement. Sagittarians can have a tendency to think more about the big picture and less about details, but it is this big-picture mentality that has helped Tyra to look beyond the runway and build a wildly successful career as an actress, television personality, spokeswoman, and supermodel. Restless Sagittarians can also have difficulty finishing things they start—but not Tyra. She has a well-developed work ethic and is very dedicated to all of her pet projects. Instead of quitting one project to begin another, she just piles them on and plows forward and doesn't stop until she's succeeded at them all.

Sagittarians always stand out in a crowd, and at almost six feet tall, Tyra can't help but get noticed. But Tyra really stands out because she is so passionate and charismatic. Tyra has very strong moral convictions, and, in true Sag fashion, is outspoken and active about the issues she feels so strongly about. Camp TZone is a perfect example of Tyra's Sagittarian passions and generosity put to good use, and through the camp, Tyra has been able to help thousands of young women improve their self-esteem and their images of themselves as women. Sagittarius is a sign associated with truth and justice, and you can bet that Tyra will spend the rest of her life pursuing justice and working toward a more truthful and positive image of women in the media and throughout the world. Using *The Tyra Banks Show* to reach a wide audience, Tyra works diligently to expose injustices in society to her viewers, like the time she wore a fat suit for a day to show just how poorly overweight people are treated on a daily basis.

When it comes to love, Sagittarians like Tyra are passionate and romantic, but their restless nature can sometimes sabotage even the best relationships. The best match for a Sagittarius like Tyra would be an Aquarius, Aries, Leo, Gemini, or even another Sagittarius. These signs like change as much as Sagittarius and can always provide enough laughter and adventure to keep Sagittarius on her toes. Tyra is one powerful woman, and she definitely needs someone who can keep up with her crazy lifestyle without being threatened by her success, which is why she probably wouldn't click quite as well with Capricorn or Taurus—those signs are too resistant to change for Tyra's Sagittarian ways—and Virgo and Pisces— two signs that require constant attention and are sticklers for rules and order.

Tyra has made some incredible friends throughout her career, but one reason that she has been so successful is her fiercely independent nature. Sagittarians love having adventures with their friends, but they also don't need anyone around to have a fantastic time. They say it's lonely at the top, but for a Sagittarius like Tyra, that isn't such a bad thing. Independent Sags enjoy time to themselves, with no one to hold them back as they flit from one thing to the next. Tyra is a born leader, and her big personality and excitement for life is contagious whenever she is in a group. Fire signs like Sagittarius tend to have the best friendships with air signs— Gemini, Aquarius, and Libra—because these signs are funny and embrace constant change but are happy to let Sagittarius take the lead, which Tyra does naturally. Other fire signs—Aries and Leo—are also good friends for Sagittarius, but those friendships tend to have more tension and drama since all fire signs like to be the center of attention and competition can arise easily when fire signs get together. The only water sign that works well with Sagittarius is Scorpio, since Scorpios are just as passionate as Sags but are mysterious and secretive enough to keep Sagittarius guessing.

Tyra Banks is a whirlwind of activity, passion, and generosity. Her star sign means that you'll never find her sitting still or taking no for an answer—no matter how tough the obstacle, Tyra is sure to overcome it. It's that Sagittarian energy and excitement for life that makes Tyra so much fun to watch, and it's her sign's constant evolution and reinvention that keeps us all coming back for more.

Chapter 23
Final Fun Facts

*B*y now you're an expert on all things Tyra, but here are some fun facts to file away. Then wow your friends with your amazing knowledge of this amazing woman!

♥ Tyra has kept a journal since the age of seven.

♥ When she was fifteen, she won tickets on the radio to attend the Soul Train Music Awards. That night, she thought she had gotten Reverend Run's autograph (from Run-DMC). Turns out it was his bodyguard's signature.

♥ She got used to doing her own makeup at fashion shows because when she started, she'd always be bumped from her place in line by a supermodel. Now she usually carries about thirty eye shadows and thirty lipsticks with her. (Talk about being prepared!)

♥ Some of her friends nicknamed her "Summer Springs" because she's always wearing clothes for warm weather—even in the freezing cold.

♥ One of Tyra's best friends is the outrageous fashion designer and model Kimora Lee Simmons. Tyra was the maid of honor at her wedding to music producer Russell Simmons.

♥ Despite her mega-fortune, she fears going broke. She'll even reuse the same tissue to remove makeup smudges for three weeks.

♥ Tyra's brother, Devin, is an air force paramedic. He was once stationed in Okinawa, Japan.

♥ Tyra's favorite food indulgence is ice cream, specifically Häagen-Dazs's coffee flavor. She forces herself to scoop it out of the pint and put it in a cup. "If I don't, I will eat the whole thing."

♥ Tyra is allergic to dogs.

♥ Tyra shelled out $30,000 of her own money to finance a music video of "Shake Ya Body," a song she recorded. The video aired during a segment of *America's Next Top Model*.

Tips on Tyra

Obviously, plenty of information on Tyra can be found online. But if you're going to surf the web, be responsible. Only use the Internet with your parents' or another adult's permission, and stick to official websites rather than fan sites, which are often unregulated.

Keep in mind that with websites, often what's here today is gone tomorrow—so get surfin' while the surf's up!

TYRA'S OFFICIAL WEBSITE

www.tyrabanks.com

A complete biography, with information on Tyra's many ongoing projects. The most comprehensive, fully authorized site out there.

THE TYRA BANKS SHOW WEBSITE

tyrashow.warnerbros.com

The official site for Tyra's talk show.

AMERICA'S NEXT TOP MODEL OFFICIAL WEBSITE

www.upn.com/shows/top_model

On this site you'll find information about the hit TV show as well as biographies and portfolios of the contestants—and their fierce hostess!